Library of Congress Cataloging-in-Publication Data

Samli, A. Coskun.
    Chaotic markets : thriving in a world of unpredictability / A. Coskun Samli.
        p.   cm.
    Includes bibliographical references and index.
    ISBN 0–275–99371–X (alk. paper)
    1. Marketing.   2. Strategic planning.   I. Title.
HF5415.S2715   2007
658.8′101—dc22   2006038661

British Library Cataloguing in Publication Data is available.

Library of Congress Catalog Card Number: 2006038661
ISBN-13: 978–0–275–99371–9
ISBN-10: 0–275–99371–X

First published in 2007

Praeger Publishers, 88 Post Road West, Westport, CT 06881
An imprint of Greenwood Publishing Group, Inc.
www.praeger.com

Printed in the United States of America

The paper used in this book complies with the
Permanent Paper Standard issued by the National
Information Standards Organization (Z39.48–1984).

10 9 8 7 6 5 4 3 2 1

D1519244

Chaotic Markets

Thriving in a World of Unpredictability

A. Coskun Samli

Westport, Connecticut
London

This book is dedicated to those who have the understanding of the chaotic nature of markets and are able to develop counterchaos strategies.

Contents

Preface

There are millions of companies in the very dynamic economy of the United States. Their primary concern is to survive. After all, if we don't survive, we cannot grow and prosper. We may not be seeking greatness, we may not be seeking maximization, but we certainly are seeking survival and a reasonable return to investment. Take a little women's apparel store with the name of Bonomo's, in a southeastern university town. The store owner had very good and artistic taste. She managed the store with an atmosphere of warmth. The ambience and the merchandise mix were all pleasing. She also had the most prominent ladies in town as part-time salespeople. These ladies had many friends. Thus, in the store the atmosphere was one long and ongoing party. Now, Bonomo's was very successful. Should this store have aimed at greatness? Probably NOT. It certainly was not the best in the world and the proprietor did not even consider such a concept. There was no piercing insight into driving the economic engine that made the store very successful. However, everybody who worked there was very friendly and deeply passionate about what they were doing. Not a world-class store, it was better than good, but not GREAT.[1] This is where most, if not all, American businesses would like to be. The proprietor of Bonomo's called her store "my little gold mine." As Collins[2] posited, out of thousands perhaps 11 are great. But literally hundreds of companies that I have known—big, small, manufacturer, wholesaler, retailer, and service—have resembled Bonomo's. Thus this book is not about greatness, but all firms can become *very good* and can achieve market power. This is the essence of market capitalism. All firms can learn to encounter chaotic market conditions and generate consumer value if they have carefully thought out and implemented market strategies. Understanding American markets is very difficult, but without such understanding, survival is impossible.

Markets are extremely dynamic and, by definition, not very friendly. The modern firm must realize that marketing problems can be solved by marketing activities, not by organizational restructuring, by some financial manipulation, or some internal musical chairs game within the company's top management.

It is not necessarily a normal phenomenon but giants such as Kodak, Sears, General Motors, or somewhat smaller firms such as American Safety Razor or Giant Foods, Inc., sooner or later have to, in fact must, hit a stone wall or a major snag in terms of changing needs, varying consumer desires, or introduction of some totally unexpected products that would make their products obsolete. It happens almost all the time. Many companies, large and small, throughout their journey in the marketplace, hit snags that can be a setback or a totally devastating experience. They lose their competitive edge, and their existence becomes threatened. Any firm, in the ultradynamic market system, must create a competitive advantage by achieving market power. Creating and maintaining competitive advantage in today's markets is so challenging that it borders on impossibility. Not only thinking out of the box, but also performing out of the box, is a necessary prerequisite not only for success but also for survival. "Business as usual" orientation is no longer acceptable. Thinking out of the box is not something that is done automatically. The firm must be doing this, on and off, powerfully and regularly. Thus, the modern firm must develop a culture of thinking unconventionally. That culture must be practiced in a disciplined manner. Without such orientation, in view of the increasing adversities of modern markets, the firm has little chance for survival.

In an earlier book, I used the concept of *value marketing*. Indeed, marketing in the final analysis is creating value; therefore, success in the marketplace is related to the success of consumer-value generation. However, generating consumer value is becoming more difficult as adversities in our markets accelerate.

This book, after many years since the earlier book, deals with the realities of chaotic markets. Here a key assumption is that market adversities are bordering on chaotic proportions. The greatest challenge for the corporate entity, therefore, is to survive chaotic shocks in the marketplace and be profitable at the same time. Surviving market shocks and remaining profitable are still equated with value generation. Hypercompetition that prevails in our markets makes generating consumer values, particularly extraordinary values, more and more difficult and, hence, survival in the marketplace due to generating extraordinary values is becoming a great challenge. Thus, today's market realities are not only very different than in the past and much more complex, but they are also much more difficult to cope with. Throughout the book, two sets of reasoning are posited. First, in order to become reasonably immune to chaotic market shocks, the firm must be futuristic, proactive, and devoid of conventional wisdom. It must be disciplined in this overall orientation of *managing the future.* Second, the firm must also manage the present and generate market power by creating consumer value as of now. Thus, the firm must manage both the present and the future. This is coined in this book as an "ambidextrousity." There is no future if the present is not managed well, but also there is no future if the future is not managed at all.

Both of these approaches, that is, managing the present and managing the future, must be juxtapositioned against the way markets are described throughout this book, *disorderly disorder.* Coping with the disorderly market is a major challenge. In fact, it is THE CHALLENGE in attempting to generate market power. But when we realize that the existing disorder, such as the unpredictability of events, sudden shock waves, unexpected developments, and the like, continue in a disorderly fashion, then the challenge becomes incomparably greater.

The modern corporate entity simply cannot afford to remain traditional, continue to be guided by conventional wisdom, and see the future as a simple extension of the present. "Business as usual" orientation not only does not work, but is also the "kiss of death."

Guided by futuristic proactivity, the firm must also develop the most suitable generic strategy for itself. A proper strategic game plan can create a sustainable competitive advantage. This will improve the firm's market position, since strong competitiveness provides certain immunity to unexpected and increasing adversities of the market.

The modern firm does not only owe it to itself to be more proactive and futuristic, but it also owes it to the society as a whole and to its customers as well. This author believes that the more consumer value is generated, the smoother will be society's desires for dramatic changes.

In some important recent research, a number of critical points have surfaced. However, these points must be carefully understood and implemented.[3] Although it has not been articulated as such, it has been implied that some leaders are *predestined* to be great. This is important, but what do we say to a struggling company? Go get yourself a predestined great leader?

Another point that has surfaced recently in management thinking is that those leaders who are modest do better. Again, first, how do we really measure modesty; second, how do we teach modesty; and third, is it really modesty or something else that creates success?

Simplification of the description of the problem appears to be advocated. First, simplicity has nothing to do with the very complex nature of the markets. Second, it is not the identification of a problem: it is getting to where the market is headed, and getting there earlier that needs to be emphasized. It must be stated at the outset that wishful thinking is NOT a strategy. There must always be a game plan or a plan of action.

Finally, "never lose faith" and "stay in there" have been advocated. Modern marketing-related issues cannot possibly be resolved with the faith to oneself and to the company alone. Market-related problems and opportunities require market-oriented activity, not just having faith in management to do things right.

All of these factors or considerations have a place and a role to play. However, first we are not trying simply to create a few "great" companies. All companies must be "great" in their own way. Second, in order to survive we must create market power. Without that there will be no future for our firm. Creating market power is a sign of greatness and cannot be achieved by looking out from the inside. Looking out from the outside is essential for achieving market power. All firms must achieve market power by generating consumer value. Here, throughout this book "consumer value generation" is used to imply that the firm is obligated to generate value not only for stockholders and stakeholders, but also for the society.

Thus, this is not a book of clichés. This is not a book of predictions; this is not a book of wishful thinking; this is not a book of forecasting the future. This is a book about thinking nonconventionally. This is a book about the modern markets, understanding them and using them proactively to generate consumer value and sustainable competitive advantage and, hence, *gaining market superiority.*

A. Coskun Samli
Ponte Vedra Beach, Florida
March 2006

Acknowledgments

A book cannot be written without the contributions of many people, and this is no exception. I may say that this book has been in the making for over 40 years, and many people directly and indirectly contributed to it. Early on, my thinking was formed by my dissertation research on business failures, under the meticulous guidance of Professor Stanley Hollander of Michigan State University. One of the best scholars of my time, a mentor, and a friend, Dr. Hollander's impact on my thinking and on my research has been rather difficult to acknowledge fairly. I owe him more than I can pay back and I miss his wisdom and friendship dearly.

My friend, colleague, and coauthor in many projects of many years, Professor Joe Sirgy of Virginia Tech, has always been available to argue or interact. His influence on my thinking has been profound. Dr. Edward Mazze, Dean of the College of Business at the University of Rhode Island, has spent much time with me on the phone discussing many related and less-related items regarding this book. Intellectually I must confess that I have been influenced by Peter Drucker's thinking and writing.

Some of my colleagues at the University of North Florida have directly and indirectly influenced my thinking. Dr. Edward Johnson, Dr. Ronald Adams, Dr. Greg Gundlach, Dr. Earle Traynham, Dr. Adel El-Ansary, and others all have been kind enough to carry on detailed conversations with me.

During my 40-year-plus professional career, I have done much research and much consulting. All of these efforts and what I have learned from them are found between the lines and pages of this book. But, above all, my weekend MBAs and my evening MBA students, most of whom are seasoned middle managers, have reacted to my ideas and interacted with me to raise the level of knowledge that we have exchanged.

At the firing line, my research assistants Tomas Miho and Sarah Forstner have given me the necessary informational inputs so that the ideas presented in this book can be further refined. Our secretaries, Leanna Payne and Carolyn Gavin not only were patient with me, but also successfully deciphered my mostly illegible handwriting. I am truly grateful for the support I have received. That also goes for my department head, Dr. Gene Baker, who helped me by not scheduling me unreasonably. As in many times in the past, Beverly Chapman gave me a helping hand in editing my manuscript. As usual, she was very helpful. Above all I would like to extend my appreciation to Nick Philipson, Senior Editor of Praeger Publishing Group, who has given me numerous valuable ideas to make this book more helpful to our readers. I am truly grateful.

To these and many other people who, over the years, discussed, interacted, or researched these issues with me, I extend my deepest gratitude. However, needless to say, I am solely responsible for the contents of this book. I sincerely hope that it makes a modest but noticeable contribution to the well-being of all of my friends in business, both those that I know and those that I have never met.

Introduction

Adam Smith could not possibly have imagined the Internet, or information technology, or modern management thinking. But, since his time, complexities of the market system have accelerated incessantly. In fact, complexities of the market system accelerate geometrically even though business populations and markets themselves grow arithmetically. But along with these complexities, adversities in the marketplace also accelerate.

The increasing adversities in the marketplace must be understood and evaluated constantly and effectively so that a firm can develop and maintain market power. The market system has multitudinous pressures, creating adversity for the modern business enterprise. Figure I.1 presents five general categories of adversity-causing pressures. These are: government and globalization, scientific progress, external uncontrollables, increasing competition, accelerating consumer demands, and external uncontrollables. These are discussed, in some detail, throughout the book. Just a brief review is in order. It must be reiterated that if these threats are not understood well, there cannot be proactive management action to enhance the opportunities for survival.

GOVERNMENT AND GLOBALIZATION

The complexities of modern living have been forcing governments to regulate, re-regulate, or deregulate and create much unwanted yet, at times, much needed controls. In recent years, these controls or lack thereof have been further modified and intensified by the globalization process.[1]

Businesses are struggling to combat fierce international competition as they also try to follow the dictates of local and national regulations.

The globalization process clearly enables the transfer of most up-to-date technology. Even though it may not be the "most appropriate" technology, it takes off successfully for a very small sector of the economy and crashes small existing businesses brutally. In Friedman's[2] terminology the global process comes on like an "electronic herd" and exerts tremendous pressure on the existing small businesses.

SCIENTIFIC PROGRESS

In addition to producing better products more efficiently, scientific progress is also creating disruptive technologies. This concept is discussed in greater detail in this book. Suffice it to say that companies quite often have difficulty deciding if they should stick to continuing technologies or switch to disruptive technologies. The latter may suddenly make the firm's products outdated, useless. Another track in scientific progress is related to information, which, again, is used by some companies, creating extremely difficult competition to cope with. Those few companies that use information technology skillfully can gain significant cost benefits against which other less skillful firms cannot compete. Similarly the future of the computer industry may be questioned as nanotechnology-related products emerge.

INCREASING COMPETITION

Increasing competition, all by itself, is a major category. Merger mania, e-trade, the outreach of global giants, and the emergence of small and medium size businesses are just a few aspects of this all-encompassing category. Not only is competition increasing because of the number and size of companies, but also because of competitive strategies and tactics.

When Johnson and Johnson acquires a new, small, but very dynamic company, it enters a new market from the high-end with significant expansion of the newly purchased company. Such activities suddenly change the nature of existing competition and make it extremely difficult for those who may take the approach of "business as usual" and have been doing business in the middle of the center of the market.

ACCELERATING CONSUMER DEMAND

When consumers wanted speed, microwave ovens as well as fast cars emerged. Consumers wanted comfort, and SUVs emerged. These are just a few examples of what this author calls "demand pull." However, consumers or the market do not have much to say about, say, the development of *nanotechnologies* or fuel cell energy research which are examples of technology push. There is a constant change and hopefully improvement in consumer products and services, provoked by the increasing level of sophistication on the part of the consumer as well as improved technology. Hence, consumer demands are accelerated by *demand pull* and/or *technology push*.

EXTERNAL UNCONTROLLABLES

As this book is being written, the American economy is in a recession. Recessions typically force many businesses out of existence. Business failures and business discontinuances are extremely costly propositions to the individual companies and to the society as a whole. Similarly the remedies, if any, which are used by the federal and state governments create pressure on different business sectors in different forms. For instance, at the writing of this book, very large tax cuts are being given to the upper one percent of the society. As a result, there may be a significant increase in demand for yachts, expensive cars, and services of Swiss banks, but the outcome of these tax cuts would not stimulate demand for K-Mart or Wal-Mart stores, since the recipients of major tax cuts do not shop in these stores. Furthermore, tax cuts will create deficits that may create a very significant financial problem in the long run. Finally, because of their consumption patterns, the rich will not run off and buy things as the people with limited means would do. Regardless of the exact outcome, recessions and the remedies used to correct them are likely to send shock waves throughout the market system.

In fact, the first four of the five pressure systems that are identified in Figure I.1 can be classified as external uncontrollables. In all of these cases, the firm does not possess any controlling or counteracting weaponry. These pressure causing factors and others are discussed in greater detail later on. However, suffice it to say here that the pressures caused by these factors are chaotic for many firms.

Pressure-causing adversity is accelerating. It is critical to develop a counteractive weaponry that will enable the firm to cope with the chaotic pressures.

Figure I.1.
Adversity-Causing Pressures.

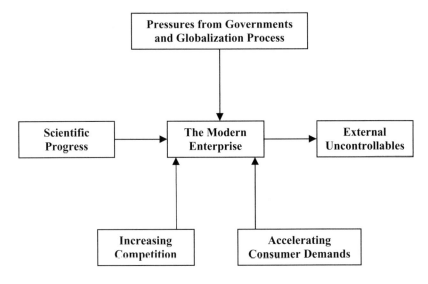

ADVERSITY IN THE MARKETPLACE ACCELERATES

Adversities are further fed by globalization, computerization, consolidation, deregulation, intellectual capital creation, and other far-reaching developments. All of these give additional boost to the adversity-causing pressures, generating a self-propelling adversity with which modern businesses must cope.

In dynamic markets of the world and particularly in those of the United States, the adversity-causing pressures have been accelerating to chaotic proportions.

- Establishing tough autosafety regulations created chaos for Volkswagen in the 1960s.
- For surgeons who are performing open surgery, the emergence of arthroscopic and endoscopic surgery created chaos.
- Currently notebook computers have experienced shock waves created by hand-held digital appliances.
- An estimated 90,000 businesses ceased to exist before the 2003 economic recession was over.

Such a list can be extended just about indefinitely, indicating the emerging chaotic conditions in the market system. As adversity reaches chaotic proportions and becomes a regular occurrence, then those businesses that are not prepared for coping with the emerging shock waves are likely to lose their footing and even their existence in the marketplace.

FROM ADVERSITY TO TURBULENCE AND FROM TURBULENCE TO CHAOS

Marketing takes place in the economy. It either moves along with current economic activity or moves against the economic tide. These two options for marketing, that is, pro- or countereconomic tide, are not of equal importance. The outcomes of the two are not likely to be equal. Moving against the economic tide is not quite an alternative, but a firm that is inactive or mildly reactive to market changes is in that position and cannot fare well against adversities. Marketing, as a very powerful process and a socioeconomic force, has to be proactive enough to decide how to deal with market adversities. If the economic tide is low, marketing needs to go against this tide proactively enough that overall economic activity is heightened. If the economic tide is high, proactive marketing may reinforce this tide and benefit fully from it.

But, in time, in a dynamic economy, the competition and conditions in the market have become more and more adverse. As the markets change from sellers' markets to buyers' markets, in other words, as the consumers start calling the shots in the market system as originally intended, the levels of market adversity continue to increase to a level of turbulence. More and more businesses are trying to get a part of the consumer dollar by offering more and more goods and services.

Samli[3] identified at least seven factors causing market turbulence. These are briefly discussed below.

Consumer Uncertainty

In the increasing complexities of the American market, consumers developed numerous uncertainties. These were based on dwindling confidence in the job market, vacillating incomes and varying qualities of goods and services, just to name a few.

Time Management

Time became more and more critical in the quality of life considerations. Consumers consider themselves constantly under serious time constraints and require more time-efficient products and services.

Market Fragmentation and Customization

The mass markets of previous eras gave way to multiple idiosyncrasy-based niche markets, and markets became fragmented. Individuals have been pushing even further to achieve customization, that is, personal attention to their particular needs. As consumer sophistication increases, such pressures become a major source of turbulence to businesses.

Quality, Design, and Service

Unlike earlier eras, as market needs changed, they changed in an intensified manner. Consumers demanded not just variety but extensive variety. They demanded not just entertainment but a wide range of entertainment. They demanded not just reasonable ovens, but superspeed microwave ovens. These intensified need changes spilled into all aspects of the market. More services, more personalized designs, more quality products are being demanded.

Insensitivity to Market Need Changes

Businesses, much of the time, started having difficulty in coping with dramatically changed and intensified market needs. Either they could not see these dramatic changes emerging or they simply encountered difficulties meeting these changes.

Insensitive Front Line Personnel

Front line personnel in businesses, by not being responsive or by not being attentive, exacerbated difficulties. They could not quite satisfy consumers' information needs. Consumers became disenchanted.

The Feeling of Losing Value

Because of the larger size of businesses due to increasing oligopolistic patterns in the market where a few businesses control a large proportion of the particular market, consumers feel small and powerless. The oligopolists who are far removed from consumers and not entirely sensitive to consumer needs, make consumers feel that they are losing value and being pushed around.

The turbulent era is still present and continuing. However, in addition to turbulence, other and more powerful adversities have emerged. Adversity-causing pressures are in chaotic proportions and creating tremendous difficulties for the modern enterprise. This book primarily deals with this extreme phenomenon even though the discussion presented throughout is also applicable to all market adversities.

Figure I.2.
Lacking Internal Sensitivity.

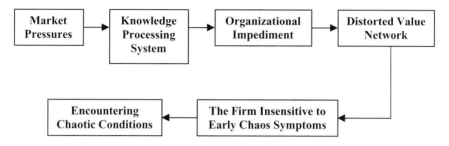

KNOWLEDGE PROCESSING SYSTEMS

Goethe, the famous German philosopher, once stated: Everyone lives, but only a few realize that they are alive. The same concept is more dramatically applicable to business. One very good explanation of why companies fail can be easily attributed to what Goethe meant—that is, companies are not aware of their own being due to what Christensen[4] calls organizational impediments. The company either does not have a *knowledge processing system* to understand what is happening in the market, or the processed knowledge does not go to the people in the organization who can do something about market adversities.

The second aspect of the above-mentioned inadequacy of the existing knowledge processing system is related to already established *value network*.[5] All firms, whether cognizant of it or not, have a value network. This is the network within which the firm identifies and responds to customers' needs, solves its problems, purchases what it needs, responds to market conditions, and generates profit. Thus, the value network is the cradle of the firm's strategic being and its functional activities. As such, the value network leads in the direction of the firm's internal reward system. The more established the firm, the more entrenched the overall processes of the firm. But, as mentioned earlier, if the knowledge processing system is somewhat dysfunctional and is not overcoming the established organizational impediments, implying that the firm is becoming less cognizant of its own existence, then disaster is likely to ensue.

Thus, if the knowledge-processing capabilities of the firm do not activate the firm's ability to understand its relationships with its markets, the firm is destined to face chaos. Figure I.2 illustrates this chaotic progression. Activating the firm's ability to counteract chaos before it happens is not wishful thinking; it is a necessity.

PROBABILITY OF CHAOS CAN BE FACED WITH COUNTERCHAOS MARKETING

Once again, we must consider Goethe. The firm must be fully cognizant of its own existence. As illustrated in Figure I.2, if the firm's internal sensitivity is less than adequate, the firm is destined for hardship in the marketplace. Continuing to function in that fashion cannot possibly lead the firm in a counterchaos path. As discussed elsewhere in this book, the firm not only should be cognizant of its existence, but also must be capable of taking dramatic action, which may not have been its traditional manner of functioning. Thus, the past, the present, and the future directions of the firm need to be identified. Understanding how the firm got where it is at that moment can be a good clue, but it is only that: just a clue. In fact, most companies that have a habit of listening to their best customers, and identifying new products accordingly, are not likely to survive in extremely dynamic markets where disruptive technologies are plentiful.[6]

Perhaps a simple analysis of Sears may explain Figure I.2. Sears, the number one retailer at the time, started feeling pressure from Wal-Mart. Its knowledge-processing system distorted its perception and led the company in the direction of numerous financial ventures. Thus, the company experienced a distorted value network. In the meantime, Sears' key target market of upper-middle-class was shrinking. Its insensitivity to early chaos symptoms led the company into the current chaotic market conditions without a vision for the future and without a focus.

As we advocate an improvement in the internal sensitivity of the modern firm, we must also illustrate how chaotic developments influence the firm and how a counterchaos marketing strategy needs to come about. Figure I.3 presents a general picture of how a counterchaos corporate strategy emerges. As seen in the Figure, chaotic influences can threaten extinction and/or promise extraordinary gains. Sears did not realize that its core market lost economic power, and thus became more cautious with its money, preferring to patronize Wal-Mart or Target where lower-priced goods are available. Sears is still under shock.

At the totally opposite end of the spectrum, Microsoft came up with its Windows series as personal computers became very popular. A shock wave served the company well. Figure I.3 shows that the firm had a swift reaction against the chaotic influences that lead to the development and implementation of strategic market plans. But if the firm interpreted the chaotic influences as not important and its current equilibrium in the marketplace as safe and sustainable, the firm would have been in great danger of becoming extinct.

Figure I.3.
The Essence of Counterchaos Marketing.

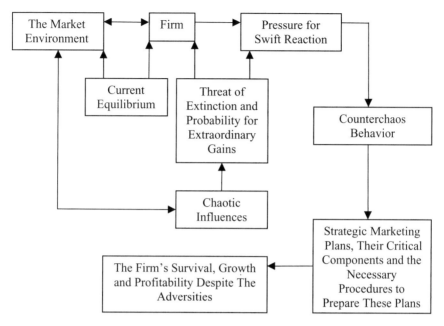

Thus, at any given time, the market and hence our firm must be functioning as expected. This may be named equilibrium. However, chaotic influences not only pressurize the firm to react swiftly, but also force the firm to understand that it is facing the threat of extinction or the possibility of making extraordinary gains. Such extraordinary gains can be the result of the firm's swift and proactive response to the dramatic market changes. Counterchaos strategies must always be on the back burner with the possibility of sudden release.

Development of such counterchaos strategies and their sudden release are all part of the core thinking in this book. Modern firms cannot survive without having certain counterchaos strategies that can be released promptly. Throughout the book there will be examples illustrating how firms can survive market shocks and convert them into opportunities.

THE FUTURE IS NOT A CONTINUATION OF THE PAST

It would not only be naïve, but downright dangerous, to assume that the firm can continue its smooth sailing in the midst of a very dynamic, if not a chaotic, market. Indeed, some years ago Drucker[7] stated: "A time of turbulence is a dangerous time, but its greatest danger is a temptation to deny reality." He observed that there is collision between the decisions of corporate management and market realities. This can easily be related to the firm's not being cognizant of its position in dramatically changing markets. If the markets are changing dramatically, how could the firm ignore the realities of the market and continue functioning under the assumption of business as usual? Market realities cannot be denied, nor can they be ignored. However, a powerful firm goes beyond acknowledging and not ignoring market realities; this is where true market leadership emerges.

THE TRUE MARKET LEADER INVENTS ITS OWN FUTURE

RCA spent millions of dollars in the mid-1930s to develop the black and white television. For years it did not receive a dime from the millions that it invested.

A distinction must be made between innovating for the future versus improving past performance.[8] In the most dynamic and unpredictable modern markets, if the companies cannot make a distinction between what is and what should be, they are not likely to survive. Emphasizing what has been practiced all along is only improving past performance, whereas emphasizing what should be is innovating for the future. For many years, IBM emphasized improving mainframes and almost lost it all because the company did not emphasize PCs soon enough. It was improving past performance as opposed to innovating for the future. Intel moved very quickly from being a "semi-conductor company" to a "microcomputer company." With such a strategic transformation, it became a leader and invented its future. Indeed, inventing the future is not an option for a leader; rather, it is a necessity if a leadership is to be established or maintained.

SUSTAINING COMPETITIVE ADVANTAGE

In extremely dynamic and unpredictable markets, maintaining competitive advantage by emphasizing what is there and improving on the past is almost an impossibility. Sears, RCA, and Kodak, among many others, have experienced a major loss in their competitive advantage mainly because they could not foresee the changes in their markets.

It is maintained here that the competitive advantage of a firm, that is, its ability to compete and its resultant market share reflecting its profitability, can be sustained only if the firm is inventing its future and managing for what it should be rather than for what is.

In a decade, the American economy can witness over 600,000 business failures and at least that many business bankruptcies.[9] Many of these businesses did not have a substantial competitive advantage, in fact that is why they are not in the market any more. The negative impact of such numbers on the economy is rather spectacular.[10] Without making an attempt to calculate individual savings, salaries, profits, and manpower that are lost, the increasing number of business failures and bankruptcies has reached chaotic proportions. The economic and societal impact of these business discontinuances are almost incalculable.

Once again it must be reiterated that a business, without being a leader in the market or in its respective industry, could easily counteract increasing adversities of the market by developing certain counterchaos strategies. Such strategies can be developed and used by all firms in the dynamic markets of modern economies. Once again, those firms may not become great but will have good returns on investments and will generate good consumer value.

SUMMARY

This chapter presents five types of adversities in the marketplace that are causing pressures on the firms that function in these markets. The adversity in the marketplace accelerates and reaches chaotic proportions. The firm must have a knowledge-processing system that leads to value networks that counteract the emerging chaotic conditions.

The firms must develop counterchaos marketing to stay alive. Such counterchaos marketing is not based on business as usual. This means the future in a dynamic market is not a continuation of the past. If the firm is a true leader, it will be able to invent its own future. This means innovating for the future rather than improving the past.

READING THROUGH THIS BOOK

The following is a brief synopsis of each chapter.

• There is a need for thinking market superiority and partially resultant counterchaos marketing strategies. The author discusses general orientation and the philosophy of the book (Preface).

- Increasing adversities of the marketplace create ever-increasing awareness of these market changes by the modern enterprise. Five major adversity-causing pressures include governments and globalization, scientific progress, increasing competition, consumer demands, and other external uncontrollables (Introduction).
- A detailed discussion of 11 chaos-causing factors is provided and is also connected to possible market opportunities (Chapter 1).
- In facing the very dynamic nature of the market, we simply cannot make progress by just taking a business-as-usual attitude. A proactive decision-making orientation is a must for the success of the modern business firm (Chapter 2).
- There is a very strong tendency on the part of firms to follow conventional wisdom and, without realizing it, to live, think, and function as they did in the past. This is the greatest danger for the modern firm (Chapter 3).
- In order to assess market changes and resultant emerging opportunities, we have to evaluate our performance in the marketplace as early as possible (Chapter 4).
- Just what are the key counterchaos marketing strategies? There are at least 11 counterchaos marketing practices. We must know how they need to be implemented (Chapter 5).
- If a company wants to be proactive and futuristic so that it can protect itself against unexpected market conditions and take advantage of emerging market opportunities, it must develop a learning organization (Chapter 6).
- A futuristic and proactive company is constantly exploring uncharted territories, hence it must develop a capability to improvise. Improvisation enables the firm to explore unusual alternatives with possible radical outcomes (Chapter 7).
- The firm's ultimate goal is to generate consumer value for which it will be rewarded in terms of profits. The firm must innovate new products and services. As the firm generates new products for the current market, it also develops a futuristic product portfolio. In developing such a portfolio, it explores prevailing megatrends (Chapter 8).
- If the firm is trying to be proactive and futuristic, it must cultivate a drive within itself to innovate. Developing a corporate culture that will support a drive to innovate is not an automatic activity: it requires much work (Chapter 9).
- In developing and implementing a drive to innovate, the firm must be able to understand and use its resources. In using its human resources, the firm will have to identify the activities that are proactive and counterchaos, and then must evaluate its core competencies. It is critical to prioritize the new core competency needs and develop them accordingly (Chapter 10).
- A proactive corporate discipline manages the future and not the past. Thus the corporate culture must have both vision and values for a futuristic stance that would generate consumer value (Chapter 11).

- In order to isolate itself (at least partially) from the harmful developments in the marketplace, the firm not only must have a counterchaos orientation but also must develop a competitive strategy that will enhance its market power (Chapter 12).
- Understanding the emerging markets calls for detecting, conversion, evaluation, facilitation, and implementation. This is how the counterchaos strategies are implemented (Chapter 13).
- The firm needs to use a supply chain to reach the market. This chain must create value for the consumer. Here agility and leanness of the firm are critical (Chapter 14).
- Finally, a major 12-point agenda is reviewed as the key tenets of this book (Postscript).

The critical counterchaos checklists presented at the end of each chapter would enable companies and executives to think out of the box.

Chapter 1

The Causes of Chaotic Pressures

In the Introduction we spent some time looking at the general picture that modern companies are facing. The adversities in the marketplace are attributed to five general groups of factors. In this chapter we explore these factors in much greater detail by increasing first their number to 11 and then having a serious discussion of each. But before anything else, it is critical that we repeat two thoughts that are introduced in the previous section. Market superiority can be established by a proactive company that is not improving past performance but innovating for the future. This is the firm that happens to invent its own future. Thus, business as usual is not an acceptable orientation. And in a possibly chaotic market, all past bets are off, and the firm is looking at what it can do the best even if it means a total change in its routine past practices. This is the type of proactive behavior that is necessary to cope with accelerating market turbulence.

CHAOS THEORY AND IMPORTANCE OF CHANGE

Joyce, Nohria, and Roberson[1] state that in every corporate boardroom the word "growth" provides excitement. Although, the managers who are discussing profitable growth are actually dreaming of bigness. Thus, they are not very realistic. In other words, the decision makers' inability to see the realities of the market coupled with the chaos-causing factors that are ignored unfortunately creates the perfect setting for very dangerous chaotic experiences. Drucker[2] has warned us about the dangers of turbulence, but went on to say: "but a time of turbulence is also a great opportunity for those who can understand, accept and exploit the new realities." This general orientation sets the tone of this book: *The counterchaos way of thinking is not only for survival but also for success.*

Although change and turbulence have not been unfamiliar for marketing practitioners,[3] the chaos theory has not found its way into market thinking. But if a discipline's basic assumptions about the realities surrounding it determine what it focuses on, and if the concept of chaos has not found its way into marketing realities, then the whole practice of marketing discipline may be in dire trouble. Strategic planning thus far has been based on the explicitly or implicitly acknowledged existence of linear relationships. It may be considered as the path of least resistance, but such linear relationships dwell upon improving the past performance rather than innovating for the future. If one were to describe the features of existing markets, both global and domestic, the following describe them best: uncertainty, open-endedness, plurality, change, and sudden shockwaves. Thus companies must learn to manage crises. In fact, well-managed companies of today are very susceptible to chaotic pressures as the emerging disruptive technologies create shockwaves throughout industries and markets.[4] This is because they are very comfortable and are not considering any dramatic changes. In this era of high-tech, disruptive technologies are likely to create havoc on companies that are dealing with sustaining technologies and trying to improve only past performance. This gives a major opportunity to those who function at the fringes of markets and create disruptive technologies that produce cheaper, simpler, smaller, easier-to-use items, and often with substantially different designs such as the small off-road motorcycles of Honda, Kawasaki, or Yamaha as opposed to over-the-road cycles made by Harley-Davidson and BMW.[5]

The chaos theory was originated to improve the understanding of volatile and dynamic systems. Chaos was defined as a pattern of behavior over time that is generated by a deterministic equation that is very sensitive to the starting conditions. Any two starting conditions will diverge exponentially over time.[6] Originally the chaos theory was developed to captivate the complex dynamics of the market system and remove its apparent randomness.

The chaos theory argues that relationships in complex systems such as markets, corporate entities, and other large organizations are nonlinear. These relationships are made up of interconnections and branching choices that create unintended and unexpected results. These make the universe unpredictable and therefore force the decision makers to think disequilibrium, not equilibrium. According to the chaos theory, the map of the future cannot be drawn because of the nonlinearity of relationships. Andrew S. Grove, the chairman of the board of Intel Corporation, states succinctly how chaos becomes a deadly power:[7]

When a change in how some element of one's business is conducted becomes an order of magnitude larger than what that business is accustomed to, then all bets are off. There's wind and then there's a typhoon, there are waves and then there's a tsunami. There are competitive forces and then there are supercompetitive forces.

He goes on to call such events "strategic inflection points." This is a time in the life of a business when its fundamentals are about to change. In other words, chaos sets in.

Thus, chaos theory necessitates a complete paradigm shift in thinking, planning, and implementing marketing strategies.

CHANGES CAN BE CHAOTIC

In market economies where change is a natural and critical ingredient, understanding what is needed to survive the expected and unexpected change and, from a business perspective, how that change can be beneficial to our organization, is an extremely critical condition for establishing market superiority and maintaining it satisfactorily.

Chaos theorists do not quite agree on the specifics of their theory. While some of them believe that chaos is orderly disorder, meaning that given conditions, at least in the long run, may be detected, others believe that it is punctuated equilibrium, meaning that the economy moves from one point of equilibrium to another and that this move creates shockwaves in markets. Yet there are others who consider chaos to be the change theory or nonlinear dynamics. From a mathematical perspective, chaos theory attempts to understand the pattern and structures behind nonlinear systems. If there is such divergence in the theoretical thinking, how can a counterchaos theory be articulated for marketing decision makers?

From a business perspective, we are not trying to explore, explain, or measure chaos; we are interested in detecting chaotic market conditions as they emerge and reacting to them successfully both in the short run as well as in the long run. From a marketing perspective, the present author believes that chaos can be detected, but it is not likely to repeat itself in an orderly manner. In other words, it is not likely that it will repeat itself in the long run. Its impact can hardly be totally assessed in advance; it does not fit into a pattern and does not have a detectable structure. And, above all, it comes very unexpectedly with tremendously destructive vigor. Thus, stated differently, unlike the claim of many, chaos is not orderly disorder but, in essence, it is *disorderly disorder*. Just what is behind this disorderly disorder? If we do not recognize the forces behind chaotic disorder in the market place, it will be very difficult to establish market power. Indeed, it may be difficult to survive in the short run, let alone the long run. Although a brief attempt is made in the introduction, here a detailed discussion is presented about causes of chaos.

CHAOS-CAUSING FORCES

Although it may not be an exhaustive list, Table 1.1 illustrates 11 important chaos-causing forces.

Globalization

This is perhaps the most far-reaching development in the world, and it is causing chaotic waves in many parts of the world. In a simple description, globalization means gaining accessibility to world markets. But in the process of entering world markets, globalization is benefiting only a few and is leaving billions of people around the world behind. It is creating a bigger gap between the rich and the poor. However, globalization can be a tremendous opportunity for third world countries and companies by which economic growth can be achieved.

Technology

Technology is perhaps the most remarkable force sending shockwaves across the global markets. The last 25 years of the 20th century particularly have been spectacular in terms of technological advances. Technology, which is the application of science to economic problems,[8] has been blooming at a rate that has not been equaled in the history of mankind. The infomedia industries such as computers, communication technology, and consumer electronics have passed the three trillion mark in the mid-1990s. In 1992 there were about 2.2 million people on the World Wide Web. One year later this number went up to 6.6 million. In 2006 this number is estimated to be over 1 billion (Internet World Stats). Cell phones, for instance, are changing the communication process among people. While this development is playing havoc with the existing communication system, it is expanding negotiation and information flow processes worldwide. This

Table 1.1
Chaos-Causing Forces and Their Impact

Chaotic Factors	Example	Impact	Opportunity
Globalization	The Internet	Modified trade conditions	Many products are sold throughout the world
Technology	The cellphone	Changed communication process among people	Expanding worldwide negotiation opportunities for more trade
Competition	The automotive industry both in domestic and international markets	Better choice at lower prices	Tremendous opportunities to improve product and services
Speed	Fax or Internet	Creation of significant efficiencies in doing business	Enhancing competitive advantage of some businesses
Complexity	Computer software	Making many hardware and software choices obsolete	Improved quality of life through the use of high-tech products
Power Structures	Results of merger mania	Makes it almost impossible for small firm to function	Power can be used for R&D and for entering other markets
Lifestyles	Low fat diet	Complete change in menus and consumption	Great opportunities for vitamins, food supplements
Downsizing	Flattening organizations	Many laid-off managers are starting their own businesses	Unexpected competition, better consumer choice in certain areas
Managerial Inflection Points	The change from mainframe to PCs	Complete change in computer industry	Great opportunities for software companies and other related businesses
Disruptive Technologies	Microminiaturized production process	Revolutionary rather than evolutionary production systems	Creating new opportunities for the connected industries
Unexpected Economic Downturns	Plant closings	Widespread negative impact on local economies	Finding new alternatives for some of these plants

Source: Adapted and revised from Samli (2006).

is certainly creating new opportunities throughout the world for numerous old and new industries. Speed and accuracy of information flow is leading in the direction of technology transfer and changing the technological make up of many industries throughout the world.

Competition

Competition, particularly in American markets, has intensified and changed its nature. Partly due to the globalization and technological advances discussed earlier and partly due to the merger mania that has been going on for at least two decades or more, competition has become more dynamic and deadly. Suddenly many traditionally well-known and well-managed businesses are disappearing. Larger and less conventional firms are emerging and chasing these traditional firms out of existence. The American automotive industry, for instance, has faced fierce foreign competition. Although it creates hardship on American companies, the increased and changed nature of competition has been giving consumers a greater choice and better products throughout the world. Enhanced competition has great potential in terms of creating new and better products and services globally. However, gaining competitive advantage and achieving market power in the face of ever-increasing competition is becoming a tremendous challenge.

Speed

Modern value chains are moving incomparably faster than the distribution systems of the past. This is just one example. Recent developments such as the facsimile or the Internet are creating significant time efficiencies for the end users as they force slower and less time-efficient competitors out of existence. Once again, competitive advantage is created by some, and shockwaves are sent to others. One other key aspect of speed is that it is accelerating the generation of new knowledge. For example, it is influencing new product development, further accelerating product life cycles, and catering to increasing time consciousness of consumers the world over. Speed-to-market is also seen as the ultimate competitive weapon by some market experts.[9]

Complexity

Complexity and paradox have been the outcome of all of the factors presented above. The status of complex organizations, that is, global giants, is such that not only do they become more complex in terms of composition and function, but they also become paradoxical in their problems in that they are being forced to become contradictory and negative in their perceptions of the regular or traditional corporate way of thinking. Complexity from corporate managerial thinking to new product development activities and use of these products are making many of the existing products and services obsolete rather quickly. But, in the meantime, improvements in end products and services are delivering a better quality of life to end users. The computer software industry, for instance, is generating many complex but very useful products that are changing consumer expectations and resultant business transactions. Complexity may lead in the direction of going against early beliefs and practices. This paradoxical behavior may be necessary in modern chaotic markets.

Power Structure

Merger mania, on one hand, and flattening tax structure, on the other hand, are leading in the direction of an accelerated power concentration. Companies that are buying out their competition are amassing much economic power. The flattening of the tax structure is creating much economic power at the top of the social hierarchy since 30 percent of $40,000 is much different than, say, 30 percent of $5,000,000. As power concentrates, both the supply and demand requirements change. On the supply side, oligopolists emerge and control a disproportionate share of the market and clearly become a menace to small and vulnerable companies.[10] Simultaneously, generating a few very rich individuals or families creates a significant change in the products or services demanded. They exert their power and take away the emphasis from products or services catered to the masses to the needs of a privileged few powerful consumers. The dramatic changes in the power structure are sending shockwaves throughout many industries.[11]

Lifestyles

In dynamic societies such as ours, lifestyles change. Changes such as becoming more health conscious can create havoc in many food and apparel-related industries. However, those who can notice these changes early and react swiftly can also enjoy tremendous opportunities the changing lifestyles are bringing about. Here, being able to predict latent needs of consumers can be very profitable. In recent years, exercise equipment, vitamins, and other food supplements are enjoying unprecedented growth in demand.

Downsizing

As corporate merger mania continues, many extremely well-qualified people are laid-off who may start good new companies. Here, the surprise effect of having new competition on an unexpected scale and in an unexpected manner can be very difficult to cope with. Even more seriously, this process would encourage the emergence of disruptive technologies. Although this process may be good for the consumer, it may create substantial turbulence in the market place, and cause serious disturbances. However, as stated earlier, this process can also cause unlimited new opportunities for businesses as well as consumers.

Managerial Inflection Points

In any management, the time could arrive when a totally dramatic decision needs to be made: IBM's going for PCs and going away from mainframes; Intel's moving away from chips to microprocessors, for example. Each time such managerial inflection points emerge, there is a chaotic set of precedence. Many factors causing the decision and the decision itself are also creating significant shockwaves within the industry or the market. In a sense, all of the factors mentioned thus far, individually or jointly, can create managerial inflection points. It must be dramatically emphasized that inflection points can be managed only by those organizations that are first powerful and adaptive, and second, that can generate a counterchaos marketing strategy. These inflection points come about rather unexpectedly and, if ignored, they can be totally destructive. A proactive counterchaos management may read the conditions at the critical point just before the firm reaches the managerial inflection point.[12] Here, despite the fact that the firm is still reasonably profitable, it disassociates itself from *sustaining technologies* and its current status of incumbency, and switches to and adopts disruptive technologies.[13]

Disruptive Technologies

As mentioned earlier, a dynamic society such as ours, which drives and is driven by technological advances, has a very close relationship to these technological developments. However, as companies get ahead by participating in these technological changes and become great, they become overcommitted to what Christensen[14] calls sustaining technologies. Hence, they ignore incremental or radical developments in the field. These incremental or radical developments become disruptive technologies and change the

Table 1.2
Examples of Disruptive Technologies

Established Technologies	Disruptive Technologies
Silver halide photographic film	Digital photography
Wire line telephone system	Mobile telephone system
Notebook computers	Hand-held digital appliances
Brick and mortar building	On-line retailing
Offset printing	Digital printing
Open surgery	Arthroscopic and endoscopic surgery
Cardiac bypass surgery	Angioplasty

Source: Adapted and revised from Christensen (2003).

nature of the whole industry. This results in the failure of the industry's leading firms. Hence, one of the most chaotic forces in the economy stems from disruptive technologies. Table 1.2 illustrates a few of these. The critical point is that these disruptive technologies send shockwaves throughout the industry and the economy. Microminiaturized production processes, for instance, are leading in the direction of the emergence of revolutionary production processes. Although such a development is causing shock for conventional companies, it is also creating unlimited new opportunities for the industries that can use these processes.

Unexpected Economic Downturns

In capitalistic systems, recessions are commonplace. Much of the time they are taken as a natural and common phenomenon. However, particularly within consumer durable goods industries, recessions play a very strong negative role because purchases of consumer durables such as automobiles, furniture, electronics, and the like can be postponed. A deep and prolonged recession can play havoc on these industries and companies engaged in these. Thus, recessions can easily send shockwaves throughout the economy.

GENERATING SHOCKWAVES IN THE MARKET

All of the factors presented in Table 1.1 and particularly those examples presented in Table 1.2, jointly or individually, send shockwaves in the market. They cause chaotic influences for the firms, industries, or economies. This list is not exhaustive. There are many other governmental, financial, and economic factors that are causing chaos at different levels in different magnitudes. As it is reiterated throughout this book, it is critical to face these chaotic circumstances proactively and effectively.

CRITICAL COUNTERCHAOS CHECKLIST

1. Do we have realistic goals about our business?
2. Do we understand that the counterchaos way of thinking is for both survival and success?
3. What are the chaotic changes in our markets that provide a real threat?
4. Can we and should we prioritize the chaos-causing forces?
5. How could we handle these forces if they become a threat?

SUMMARY

An attempt is made in this chapter that, unlike chaos theory scholars, a marketing scholar would consider chaos to be disorderly disorder. Again, from a marketing perspective, that disorderly disorder could strike at any unexpected time. It cannot be avoided but with early detection it can be coped with.

Our dynamic market system creates chaotic conditions that must be identified and counteracted. Then major factors causing chaotic conditions are identified and discussed in this chapter. Eleven such factors that cause chaos are listed. There are other governmental, financial, and economic factors that may cause chaos. Of the chaos-causing factors, disruptive technologies and managerial inflection points are given more emphasis in our discussion. It must be reiterated that the list of chaos-causing factors is not exhaustive. There are and there will be unexpected factors emerging and causing chaos.

Chapter 2

Past Strategies Were Good, But . . .

It is extremely easy to think that the strategies that were successful in the past will continue to perform the same way in the future. But that is only wishful thinking. It is always important to understand how we got here. And, indeed, without such knowledge we may have no place to go. However, just to think that we can continue the way we have been doing things is a mistake. Turock[1] calls this the fatal assumption. In fact, many decision makers cannot admit that this is their assumption or, worse yet, they may not be aware of the fact that they are functioning on the basis of such an assumption.

In a constantly changing society, the fatal assumption that a past strategy will work again can cause a customer to leave the company because it is no longer addressing his or her changing needs. As a continuation of this assumption, trying to squeeze the last dollar out of an old product or service would not pay in the long run. When discount stores emerged, department stores ignored their presence and their appeal to certain consumer markets. They continued "business as usual" and lost a major portion of their total business. At the present time iPods are turning the music production industry upside down. Only those who react and manage this shock positively will survive. One point is clear: *business is not as usual in that industry.*

In the introduction of this book, an attempt is made to enforce the idea that the future in a dynamic market cannot be the continuation of the past, and moreover, that market leaders invent their future. Thus, those who think in the general framework of business as usual and who follow the continuation of past practices cannot be true leaders in the market and invent their own future. A very distinct dichotomy appears to be in existence

Table 2.1
The Dichotomous Orientations

Business As Usual Orientation	Proactive Decision-Making Orientation
Thrive on past trends	Use imagination and current information
Believe in not changing	Believe in being the first mover
Always look back to good old days	Concentrate on the future and manage for it
React to current trends	Anticipate trends and accelerate them further
Worry about markets becoming saturated	Constantly look for new opportunities
Deal primarily with sustaining technologies	Inclined to deal more with disruptive technologies
Try to improve the present performance	Innovate for the future
Conventional wisdom prevails	Unconventional wisdom is the key
Staying with the existing industry group	Break away from the pack swiftly
Wait-and-see orientation	Early calculation of risks
Risk evasion as much as possible	Risk perception, taking, and managing
Heavy involvement in current problems	Understanding future opportunities
Conventional reasoning based on high probabilities	Nonconventional thinking based on the parameters of possibilities

Source: Adapted and revised from Turock (2002) and Christensen (2003).

and needs to be more carefully analyzed. This dichotomy revolves around traditionalists and futurists. Needless to say, it is not the traditionalists but proactive futuristic leaders that can survive the negative implications of chaotic changes in the market. It is quite clear that traditionalists who make the fatal assumption are not likely to survive chaos that is created in the market.

THE DICHOTOMY

Table 2.1 illustrates some of the key differences in orientation between the traditionalists and proactive leaders. Business-as-usual orientation or the orientation of traditionalists is led by thriving on past trends. This implies that they do not believe in changing unless they have to. They try to continue as is and improve nominally at the edge if needed. They look back and not forward in terms of the company's performance and its market position. Instead of riding the current waves of market change, they react, but here they do not react immediately and certainly they do not receive the benefits of "first mover advantage," which implies that those who can move early and effectively can take advantage of the emerging new trends in the market or those who invent a breakthrough product enjoy tremendous returns to their investments. On the other hand, the traditionalists may worry about the fact that their market is or may be saturating; they do not do much about it until it is rather too late. Because of the fact that they are doing reasonably well so far, they emphasize what they are doing. Traditionalists try to do more with the same technologies, which is named here "sustaining technologies." These technologies improve the performance of the established products that account for the firm's current market position. Thus, traditionalists are likely to improve the established products only on an incremental basis and in a very modest manner. In essence, what they are doing is attempting to improve upon the past performance marginally without any dramatic changes or deviations. They stay with their industry until almost the bitter end. They follow a wait-and-see attitude. Since the traditionalists are extremely involved in current problems, they do not look elsewhere. They use conventional wisdom by looking at high probabilities based on past experiences. All in all, this group of decision makers functions on the basis of *conventional wisdom*. It is obvious that following such a comfort zone can easily make a business vulnerable to chaotic developments in the market. Sull[2] describes traditionalists as sufferers from "Active Inertia." This is a trap that creates blinders for the management; it makes the firm's resources almost worthless, creates senseless routines, makes shackles out of functional relationships, and generates dogmatic behavior. Examples of active inertia suffering are plentiful. For example, major airlines such as Delta and American, in time, have gotten stuck with their hub systems, which served them well at the beginning but created inflexibility later on. IBM's dependency on mainframes nearly destroyed the company. Compaq managers were committed to certain routines that made it impossible for the company to acknowledge market changes. The relationships of Firestone and Ford became quite dysfunctional. Sears' traditional emphasis on financial issues almost destroyed the company. These examples could go on and on.

The second set of factors, describing the proactive decision-making orientation, starts with the use of imagination and current developments in the market revealed by current information flow from the market. Proactive decision-makers do employ early intuition based on early hints of chaotic market events. Believing in and trying to be the first mover is the essence of the proactive decision-making orientation. Obviously, this necessitates concentrating on the future and managing it. Managing the future is innovation. The proactive decision-maker is ready and able to innovate products or services that no one else had even imagined. When the president of Sony visited the United States and saw people jogging, skateboarding, or skating, he raised the question, "Aren't they bored?" As an answer, Walkman came into being. Similarly, anticipating trends and accelerating them further is proactive. Having the sense, maturity, and intuition to anticipate trends and become a part of accelerating them further is the epitome of proactive behavior. Constantly looking for new opportunities, 3M Company has come up with numerous successful new products. Apple brought out iPod that plays videos as well as music. It is likely to change how people entertain themselves.

Of course, proactive decision-making is sensitive to newly emerging technologies that make sustaining technologies outmoded in time. Such disruptive technological advances do not go unnoticed. On the contrary, the company that is run proactively would embrace such technologies and run with them as quickly as possible. Thus, they innovate for the future or adopt futuristic innovations quickly. The proactive management groups swiftly break away from the pack and make their own moves. This is, of course, based on their ability to calculate the perceived risks early. This enables them to understand future opportunities. All in all, proactive decision-making processes pay much attention to unconventional wisdom. They can determine the parameters of emerging possibilities. They are therefore at the cutting edge of market changes, and they are bound to establish extraordinary market power for themselves.

CAN WE SUSTAIN OUR COMPETITIVE ADVANTAGE?

Indeed, can we sustain our competitive advantage? Certainly not by employing the fatal assumption that what worked in the past will work again. As companies rely on PCs rather than mainframe computers, on on-line stock brokerage rather than full-service stock brokerage, or on digital printing rather than offset printing, disruptive technologies are gaining momentum. Certainly in most of the cases where sustaining technologies are primarily emphasized, it is difficult to predict that a company can sustain its competitive advantage. Continuation of past practices and their replication as new situations emerge is basically choosing the *path of least resistance.* Just because certain strategies have been successful thus far is not an indication of their being successful in the future or in new and emerging situations in the markets that require special action. As we become a little more suspicious of past strategic patterns and as we find ourselves in new situations, it is critical that we be engaged in trendsetting.

TRENDSETTING IS NEEDED

Those who use the business-as-usual orientation are very familiar with the current status of their businesses; however, they lack the vision of what their businesses should become or indeed may be forced to become. They have difficulty associating their businesses with the facts of the market. Under static conditions where markets are not displaying an immediate tendency to change, their lack of concern about what their businesses should become is not serious. But this is not appropriate for our dynamic markets and the problems and rewards they offer. What if we are a major automaker and have not paid much attention to "fuel cell" technology, which displays a tremendous future for satisfying the everincreasing fuel need of society? Trying to improve our past performance would do us no good. To be sure, we will feel like buggy producers felt when the horseless buggy (automobile) was introduced. Instead, we should be in the trendsetting seat by creating the first or the best fuel cell-propelled automobile.

In setting trends, it is necessary to be futuristic. According to rumors, when Wayne Gretzky, the famous ice hockey player, was asked what it would take to become a successful player like himself, he responded by saying that one must learn not to go where the puck is, but where the puck is likely to be. A proactive and counterchaos marketing orientation also ideally must apply to the Gretzky rule. Being able to predict where the market is headed and being there before the market reaches that destination is what being a *trendsetter* is all about.

If the current management is more "business as usual" oriented, it is not likely to be a trendsetter. Not only is the trendsetter managing the future, but quite often it is also enjoying the advantages of being the *first mover.* But the first prerequisite here is to be proactive or futuristic.

Figure 2.1 illustrates this very important point; that is, in order to manage or innovate the future, which is the essence of counterchaos marketing, the management must have a proactive orientation. But having the proper proactive orientation is not enough. The management of the firm must develop a strategic foresight that will enable the company to strategically

Figure 2.1.
Orientation for Market Leadership.

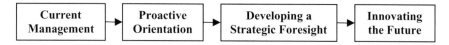

manage critical changes in the marketplace. Certainly this strategic foresight would enable the firm to innovate in the future. Being in charge of its destiny toward the envisioned future would give the firm a certain type of immunity against chaotic changes in the economy.

Developing foresight necessitates the proper proactive orientation that many companies do not possess because their managements are simply not adequately market-oriented. Quite often managements have finance or accounting backgrounds and are not intimately close to the market. Financial interpretations of the events and changes in the marketplace are very different from those of marketing interpretations.

The finance people, first, are much more prone to go for more secure undertakings. However, such orientation would prevent the firm from having the advantages of being the first mover. Second, executives with primarily financial backgrounds are not quite savvy about consumer behavior and the forces influencing consumption patterns. Finally, executives with a primarily financial background are not trained to detect market trends. Thus, unless a special provision is made in the organizational makeup, the necessary ingredients to develop a market-based strategic foresight are not present. Such a situation can make the firm unnecessarily vulnerable to chaotic developments in the market.

WHERE ARE THE LATENT NEEDS?

In a market economy, by definition, giving customers what they want is the essence of survival. Customers may express their needs through focus groups, market research, suggestion boxes, complaints, conversations at trade shows, and the like.[3] But customers or consumers in general are not visionaries. They could not have said "*give me a horseless buggy,*" "*why don't you deliver pizzas to homes,*" "*develop an internet so that I can communicate with the whole world,*" or "*develop an iPod that plays videos as well as music.*" This list could go on just about forever.

Just how can we give customers what they need if they are not articulating, indeed, if they don't know their deep-down needs? Successful marketing is giving consumers products or services they did not think they needed, but now that they have them they cannot do without these products or services. In other words, there is a huge difference between the needs consumers articulate and the needs they don't know exist. In innovating the future, latent needs are far more important than articulated needs.

Here are a few emerging consumer trends that may have given Domino's the idea to start a home delivery business.

- Consumers were facing serious time constraints.
- Two paycheck families were becoming numerous.
- Traffic on the streets at dinnertime was too heavy.
- Consumers were cooking at home less and less.
- Home cooking was not only difficult but also too time-consuming.
- Going out to eat was becoming too costly.

These conditions, and perhaps others, would be all conducive to introduce a fast, good, and reasonable home delivery system of pizza. Without developing an affinity for determining latent needs, it will not be possible to develop a strategic foresight (Figure 2.1).

From the Domino's example above, at least three principles toward determining latent needs emerge. First, major market patterns and developments must be detected. Emergence of two paycheck families, being time-pressured or having very difficult traffic congestions, for instance, are examples. Second, the far-reaching implications of these emerging patterns must be evaluated and translated into possible business propositions. Third, it must be possible to prioritize and to determine the possible size of the emerging market. Although some experts maintain that "you cannot measure a market that is not there," it is possible to estimate what proportion of the eating-out business can be replaced by pizza delivery and how big this market can be.

It is clear that the business must go where the latent needs are. The Gretzky principle that was articulated earlier was used successfully by Domino's. Without the Gretzky principle it will not be possible for the firm to develop a strategic foresight. Perhaps one thing needs further clarification. Foresight is not a forecast. Going back to Figure 2.1, the business-as-usual orientation, in an attempt to improve past performance, uses many forecasts. The proactive decision-making orientation, on the other hand, in order to innovate for the future, would employ strategic foresight. This is getting away from conventional wisdom and detecting the invisible. In other words: *thinking out of the box.*

CONVENTIONAL WISDOM

Many years ago the famous economist, John Kenneth Galbraith,[4] coined the concept of *conventional wisdom*. Because of familiarity, acceptability, and traditional thinking within the box, it is difficult to think out of the box and interpret social and economic developments in a nonconventional manner. Such a traditional approach to thinking and interpreting just what is happening in the market does not lend itself to developing the strategic foresight that would enable the firm to manage the future and hence reduce its vulnerability to chaotic developments. Perhaps the worst kind of conventional wisdom in marketing is the tendency to try to get the last mile out of an old product line instead of canning it and developing a new and more appropriate product line for the market.[5] In other words, cannibalizing your own product before a competitor does it. With the resources that are freed because of the elimination of already dying product or product line, the firm can make major progress in the market. The first column in Figure 2.1 depicts conventional wisdom as an encompassing orientation. Although a book could be written based on this exhibit, it is assumed that its details are self-explanatory, and some of its key aspects are dealt with throughout the book.

If the firm is using a proactive decision-making orientation, then it will develop a strategic foresight regarding what the future may look like and then innovate its own future as seen in Figure 2.1. In some sense, this is not only going where the puck is going to be but also being able to decide where the puck should be.

THE GILLIS CASE

Gillis has been an ice cream parlor in a southeast university town. Although it has been known for its high-quality ice cream, because of the shortness of the ice cream consumption season, the rest of the year the ice cream parlor has been rather inactive, thus the overall profitability is rather questionable. Although Gillis tried to stimulate business by improving its ice cream offering and adjusting its prices, there has been no progress in profitability.

The owner manager decided that the business must have a different orientation. With some 30,000 students and a similar number of townspeople, Gillis assumed that something over and beyond ice cream could make an impact. Gillis took a slightly countercultural path and developed very unusual and exotic soups and sandwiches. It developed a permanent display of the artwork of young artists. By approaching the problem as the future is not a continuation of the past, Gillis did very well.

CRITICAL COUNTERCHAOS CHECKLIST

1. What do we mean by "business as usual" orientation?
2. How can we create a proactive decision-making orientation?
3. Can we truly innovate our own future?
4. Does knowing how we got here imply we are tied down to those past practices?
5. Which past practices are the most serious hindrances to the future progress?

SUMMARY

This chapter begins with the fatal assumption that the practice or strategies worked in the past are bound to work in the future as well. Businesses that try to improve past performances, business as usualists, are compared to those who are proactive and managing their future rather than extending the past.

Although important, within itself, the traditional orientation is not enough. The firm must develop a strategic foresight to innovate and manage the future. Here it was reiterated that the company must be more concerned with the latent needs of the market and must go for those. Here the greatest danger is to suffer from conventional wisdom and not being able to see some of the unexpected market developments as great opportunities. The petroleum lobby may be powerful enough to disrupt the development of alternative fuels in the present time, but sooner or later it will lose that power and will be devastated. Past strategies may have been good for the past, but they may be dangerous for the future.

Chapter 3

Conventional Wisdom—Not

Most companies have certain products or services by which they do reasonably well. But markets change, consumers need change, and technologies change. Much of the time these companies try to improve their present performance based on their past experiences. This is because it is what they know best and it is the *path of least resistance*. In other words, they live in the past. In so doing, they continue supporting, first and foremost, their flagship products and services. As they do that, they are prone to sustaining these products and services while overlooking changes in the market. These changes may be very small and insignificant at the beginning, but they may expand very rapidly and unexpectedly.

Furthermore, as firms double their efforts to provide products or services better than their current competitors in order to establish greater market power and competitive edge, they may start "overshooting" their markets.[1] The products and services become more than what their markets need or want. This is where companies start replacing *market truths with corporate convenience.* This is an important manifestation of vested interests on the part of the company. In corporations, familiarity, typically, is the essence of acceptability. In fact, Galbraith[2] maintains that acceptability of ideas creates stability. Thus a company may settle into a dangerous pattern of *conventional wisdom* and becomes very vulnerable to chaotic developments in its markets.

CONVENTIONAL WISDOM-DRIVEN VALUES

If the company functions on the basis of conventional wisdom, certain values will emerge. These values invariably influence the company's

ideas that will lead to critical breakthrough products. As discussed earlier, latent needs cannot be articulated and, hence, consumers are not necessarily the best source of information. If our company does not pay attention to latent needs but our key competitors do, it will simply be a short time before they become superior and we will be forced to abandon our operations.

Paying Attention to Our Existing Markets Only

Although it is important to pay attention to our markets, this should not be done at the expense of ignoring everything else. If the auto industry had not paid attention to increasing demand for SUVs, it would have missed a major source of income. However, at the writing of this book, the gasoline prices have reached an all-time high, indicating a latent need for a vehicle driven by something other than gasoline. It remains to be seen if this latent demand becomes the focal force for automotive demand.

Self-reliance on Research

Research, being a scientific undertaking, is typically perceived to be an objective and unbiased source of data from which necessary information is generated. But, unfortunately, corporate research is not typically objective and unbiased. On the contrary, corporate research can be utilized as a tool by corporate management to reflect management's position on many issues and to reiterate corporate culture and its values.

Corporate culture can have two profound ways of influencing research: first, the way research questions are formulated, and second, the way research findings are interpreted. In terms of questions, those that do not have answers are more important. They unearth latent consumer needs and innovations. Conventional wisdom-guided questions may have an "I know it all" type of orientation that does not lead to the needed progress. "What do customers like about our product?" referring to a product that may have passed its maturity stage in its life cycle, certainly will not yield as good a result as asking "What do customers need other than our product?"

Interpretation of research findings similarly can create a dichotomy based on corporate culture or the research division's orientation. We should recall an old story that deals with the representatives of two shoe companies who were sent to the USSR right after World War II to explore market opportunities. The representative of the first company sent the corporate headquarters a telegram that said: "Let us not bother with this market, just

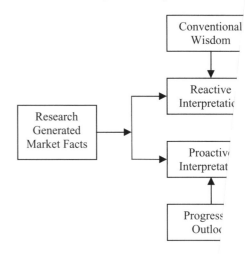

Figure 3.1.
Dichotomous Impact of Corporate Culture

about every other person wears shoes." telegram that said: "This is a gold mine. C As can be seen, the interpretation of re wisdom-driven atmosphere may not de of new opportunities. However, in a p findings may be more conducive to ide tunities. Figure 3.1 illustrates this di wisdom-driven research can be totally l ket opportunities. Contrariwise, proac research toward identifying new and e

Being Enthusiastic about Existing

Certainly a company should not ucts and services that it does not b However, within the constraints of c an overbearing orientation, leadin orientation wherein a firm puts m products rather than keeping an op ket needs for new and different pro instance, if Levi Strauss had put al blue jeans, it might have lost much jeans.

The busine *are doi* that Ri we are posited in the f of mon interpr the exist leads to favored technica address. consume

Doing

Once box. If wl more of i would no believes i future wil more than the marke the time o developed fact that th

We Must

When IB blaming the were havin its money's better if it fast-emergi product by is incompar competitors

Table 3.1
Conventional Wisdom-Driven Corporate Behaviors

Corporate Thinking	Dangerous Outcomes
• We give customers what they want.	Ignoring some of the new developments in the market.
• We don't worry much about small emerging markets. They cannot support our business.	The company can be ousted by an unexpected development.
• If the markets do not exist, we don't need to analyze them.	Emergence of possibe extremely powerful markets is ignored.
• We have the capability to carry on all the research we need.	Inherent capabilities of the company are closely related to the existing corporate culture.
• We are very enthusiastic in improving our products.	The products can become too technical and burdensome for market needs.
• We are doing well. What we need is to do more of it.	Overfocusing on the past and present.
• Let us get our money's worth from the existing ones before we start developing other products.	Missing the opportunity to enter new and profitable developments.

Source: Adapted and revised from Christensen (2003).

performance. Thus, conventional wisdom corporate values must be well understood. They typically make the organization very susceptible to chaotic market influences.

Table 3.1 presents seven elements of corporation conventional wisdom. These are the articulations of column 1 of Table 2.1. In extremely dynamic markets and industries, such sets of values and such sets of thinking leading to critical corporate strategic decisions are dangerous, to say the least.

Giving Customers What They Want

If customers could articulate their needs, better yet, if they knew their needs, this orientation would be good. In fact, clearly articulated customer needs and complaints should never be ignored. However, as stated earlier, it is quite doubtful that Henry Ford got his ideas from irate consumers who insisted on having a horseless buggy. Going where the market will go is necessary, but much of the time consumers are not the source of important ideas that will lead to critical breakthrough products. As discussed earlier, latent needs cannot be articulated and, hence, consumers are not necessarily the best source of information. If our company does not pay attention to latent needs but our key competitors do, it will simply be a short time before they become superior and we will be forced to abandon our operations.

Paying Attention to Our Existing Markets Only

Although it is important to pay attention to our markets, this should not be done at the expense of ignoring everything else. If the auto industry had not paid attention to increasing demand for SUVs, it would have missed a major source of income. However, at the writing of this book, the gasoline prices have reached an all-time high, indicating a latent need for a vehicle driven by something other than gasoline. It remains to be seen if this latent demand becomes the focal force for automotive demand.

Self-reliance on Research

Research, being a scientific undertaking, is typically perceived to be an objective and unbiased source of data from which necessary information is generated. But, unfortunately, corporate research is not typically objective and unbiased. On the contrary, corporate research can be utilized as a tool by corporate management to reflect management's position on many issues and to reiterate corporate culture and its values.

Corporate culture can have two profound ways of influencing research: first, the way research questions are formulated, and second, the way research findings are interpreted. In terms of questions, those that do not have answers are more important. They unearth latent consumer needs and innovations. Conventional wisdom-guided questions may have an "I know it all" type of orientation that does not lead to the needed progress. "What do customers like about our product?" referring to a product that may have passed its maturity stage in its life cycle, certainly will not yield as good a result as asking "What do customers need other than our product?"

Interpretation of research findings similarly can create a dichotomy based on corporate culture or the research division's orientation. We should recall an old story that deals with the representatives of two shoe companies who were sent to the USSR right after World War II to explore market opportunities. The representative of the first company sent the corporate headquarters a telegram that said: "Let us not bother with this market, just

Figure 3.1.
Dichotomous Impact of Corporate Culture on Research.

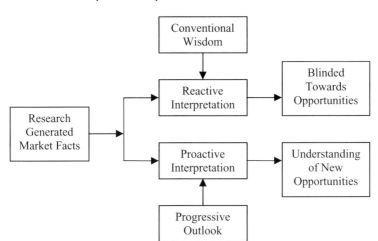

about every other person wears shoes." The second representative sent a telegram that said: "This is a gold mine. Only every other person has shoes." As can be seen, the interpretation of research findings in a conventional wisdom-driven atmosphere may not detect the presence or the emergence of new opportunities. However, in a proactive atmosphere, the research findings may be more conducive to identifying new and emerging opportunities. Figure 3.1 illustrates this dichotomous situation. Conventional wisdom-driven research can be totally blinded toward identifying new market opportunities. Contrariwise, proactive corporate culture can accelerate research toward identifying new and emerging market opportunities.

Being Enthusiastic about Existing Products

Certainly a company should not be producing and marketing products and services that it does not believe in or is not enthusiastic about. However, within the constraints of conventional wisdom, this can become an overbearing orientation, leading to what Kotler[3] would call product orientation wherein a firm puts much more emphasis on certain existing products rather than keeping an open mind, listening, and exploring market needs for new and different products for common consumer goods. For instance, if Levi Strauss had put all of its efforts into producing traditional blue jeans, it might have lost much in this age of new and more fashionable jeans.

The message here is not that the company should not focus on its core business. Indeed, Ries[4] stresses that success is *getting ingrained in what you are doing*. But clearly identifying what business we are in precedes the focus that Ries[5] talks about. What if we do not clearly identify what business we are in? Levitt[6] in his important article discussed *marketing myopia* and posited that until the motion picture industry realized that it is not really in the filmmaking business but in the entertainment business, it lost a lot of money. Conventional wisdom, quite likely, forces research findings to interpret the data in a rigid and myopic way and hence overemphasizes the existing products. Indeed, Christensen[7] maintains that this orientation leads to sustaining technologies overburdening some of the existing and favored products to become overemphasized and, hence, to become too technical and overwhelming for the market needs they were meant to address. In other words, the products become too technical and overkill consumer needs.

Doing More of What We Do

Once again, conventional wisdom encourages us to think within the box. If what we have done has brought us to where we are, we should do more of it. But, overfocusing on the past and present, at best, is reactive. It would not help us to be a trendsetter and innovate our future. If everybody believes in and does what we are doing, our chances for profit in the future will diminish considerably. We must explore what needs to be done more than what we are doing now. Despite the uncertainties that exist in the marketplace, it is critical to develop multiple futuristic scenarios. At the time of writing of this book, some Japanese automakers have already developed a prototype that runs on fuel cell-generated energy, despite the fact that these prototypes cost millions of dollars to develop.

We Must Get Our Money's Worth

When IBM declined to acknowledge the powerful insurgence of PCs, blaming the weaknesses in the world for the troubles that its mainframes were having during the late 1980s and early 1990s, it was trying to get its money's worth.[8] Certainly the company could have done considerably better if it had abandoned mainframes and assumed leadership in the fast-emerging PC market. It is quite possible that cannibalizing one's own product by killing it early before it is too late can be profitable. In fact, it is incomparably more reasonable to kill our product ourselves before our competitors do it to us.

EXTENDING THE PRESENT IS NOT ENOUGH

If the company is extending the present as a result of conventional wisdom, it is not developing the foresight needed to manage the future. Only in static markets, and indeed there is no such thing, the future is a natural extension of the past. The more volatile the market conditions, the more a company needs to manage the future, but this may not be likely under conventional wisdom-driven management thinking.

Perhaps one of the worst practices under conventional wisdom orientation is the concept of: "We tried that and it does not work." Even if a forward-looking idea has been tried in the past and did not do too well, the overall management orientation is such that it should never be tried again. If such an approach prevailed in the company's management group, Volkswagen Beetle, for example, would not have come back. Typically the "we tried that and it does not work" orientation is applied to even a new idea. If management has the orientation of "we are doing well and we don't need any change," then "we tried that and it does not work" is a natural outcome. Such an orientation totally stifles the proactive way of thinking and managing the future. However, if management is oriented to conventional wisdom and market conditions get rougher, companies resort to serious organizational change and cost-cutting activity. What we have seen during the past few years of the 21st century has been downsizing, cost cutting, and moving manufacturing facilities to offshore locations. These are belated reactions and do not represent the proactive behavior that is desperately needed. When GM faced keen competition in the late 1980s and early 1990s, it laid-off tens of thousands of workers. Sears tried to become a discounter like Wal-Mart or K-Mart, doing away with customer services provided by in-store salespeople and laying off thousands of its workers. Such a list can be extended indefinitely. Companies that cannot act proactively are forced to react by using extreme measures reflected by organizational changes. But negative developments in the market may not be of long duration and also may change again in almost the opposite direction. But organizational changes are for the long duration and cannot be changed, reversed, or eliminated quickly.

WHAT CONVENTIONAL WISDOM BRINGS

All in all, as can be seen from our discussion thus far, conventional wisdom breeds smugness, too much attachment to past and present, and only delayed and dramatic organizational responses to market changes.

Figure 3.2.
The Aftermath of Conventional Wisdom.

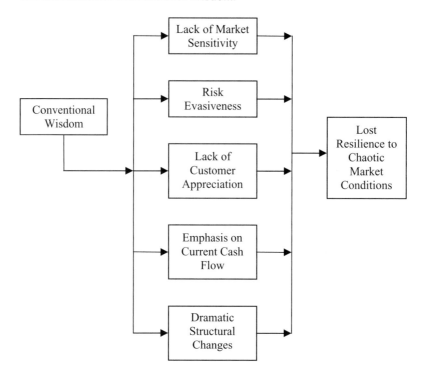

Such behavior creates five special aftermaths to which much attention needs to be paid: sensitivity, risk management, customer relations, cash flow, and structural changes.   Figure 3.2 illustrates these five aftermaths.

Lack of Market Sensitivity

Not being sensitive enough to market trends and detectable changes is not dangerous for survival but is a major deprivation of newly emerging opportunities. When many manufacturers refused to sell to discount stores because they assumed that these stores would not remain in business long, they lost much money and market leadership opportunities. Similarly in the mid-1980s, American Airlines decided to initiate a frequent flyer program. They first approached American Express. American Express did not want to share its corner of the market with another strong brand name. Nor did it want to pay the miles earned by card members. It was decided that it would be too costly. The offer was rejected. American Airlines approached Citibank. They brought out a cobranded airline mileage. The result was about $24 billion a year, a large portion of which came from American Express' earnings. Up to that point, American Express had positioned its charge card for business executives and assorted high rollers, which generated considerable prestige. But business executives decided that a bank card that rewards them with free trips is very desirable. American Express lost a lot of opportunities. These are only two of thousands of similar examples.

Risk Evasiveness

Conventional wisdom pushes in the direction of proceeding with only almost sure things and hence avoiding new opportunities because they are considered too risky. If risk is not taken, it is not possible to become the beneficiary of first-mover advantages.

Lack of Customer Appreciation

Insensitivity to changing customer needs to target market compositions and sometimes all-important customer services can be extremely risky. If the company is proceeding on conventional wisdom, it may be impossible for it to change gears and pay much more attention to what the customers are saying.

Emphasis on Cash Flow

In the early 1980s, the concept of bottom line and cost cutting became particularly important. Many corporations that were run by finance people started having plans to cut expenses upfront. Orders such as "we will cut our marketing expenses by 10 percent and increase our market share by 15 percent" became reasonably common. However, the practice orientation maintains: *managing not for a bottom line but by a bottom line*, which is a totally questionable orientation because it sets the parameters upfront and takes away flexibility. It is critical to realize that it may be necessary to spend money to make money. Particularly, it may take an increase in marketing expenses to develop a 15 percent increase in the market share rather than a 10 percent decrease in marketing expenses. Managing for a bottom line implies proactivity, which traditionalists do not have.

Dramatic Structural Changes

As was implied earlier, conventional wisdom-driven corporations may not respond to increasing market pressures until it is rather late. At such points, the chaotic shock waves from the market are counteractive with major changes in the organizational structure. Market pressures need to be encountered not by structural changes but by marketing reactions. Market conditions may change quickly, but structural changes in the corporate organization cannot be altered or eliminated quickly. Thus, conventional wisdom begets unnecessary and dangerous inflexibility by encouraging serious structural changes.

KINKO'S SECRET

Kinko's made a tremendous showing in the 1970s and onward. Trying to help professionals and students, the company established the concept that an office does not have to be a fixed facility. Instead, it can be anywhere where the necessary work is done. Considering the need of faster-flowing information and necessary paperwork in terms of reports and high-quality copies, the company focused on customer relationship management, cut costs, increased efficiency, and created a powerful and profitable organization based on the pressures and adversities of the market.[9]

CRITICAL COUNTERCHAOS CHECKLIST

1. Are we sensitive to the difference between market truths and corporate convenience?
2. Do we have conventional wisdom-driven values?
3. Just what business are we in?
4. Are we ingrained in the core business we are in?
5. Can we do well if we continue what we have been doing thus far?

SUMMARY

Conventional wisdom is the key force behind the behavior of those companies that are past- or present-oriented. It is the path of least resistance and leads in the direction of replacing market threats with corporate convenience. Certain conservative smugness prevents many companies from developing the future. Conventional wisdom determines what the company gives to its customers, how much attention it pays to market changes early on, if it predicts markets, the type of research that is undertaken, whether extra emphasis is placed on existing products, smugness about the company's market position, and the effort it will expend to get as much revenue as possible from existing products.

Conventional wisdom, therefore, creates market insensitivity, risk evasiveness, lack of customer appreciation, putting too much emphasis on the current cash flow, and dramatic structural changes. Being proactive and futuristic, it is maintained, is better than being reactive, tied down to the past and present. It is maintained that conventional wisdom weakens the company's resilience to chaotic influences in the marketplace.

Chapter 4

Early Performance Assessment
As a Start

In Chapter 3, it is indicated that the firm must not be tied to extending the present. It must be futuristic, and the future is not an extension of the past in a constantly changing market. Because of varying conditions in our dynamic market system, most firms must have a way of evaluating performance. Conventional wisdom, coupled with the orientation that concentrates on the present, necessitates much emphasis on performance evaluation. However, futuristic orientation, coupled with proactive behavior, goes much beyond the market performance evaluation and involves considerable analysis of key market forces and market developments. Thus, in marketing diagnosis, we may make a distinction between *symptoms* and *indicators*. While symptoms present assessment of current performance, indicators are future evaluation of certain events, based on their current status, which show what may happen to a business.

This distinction is rather subjective. The most important point to understand here is that evaluating our performance early on is important, but it is still an extension of the past. As opposed to evaluating the firm's performance, understanding the far-reaching implications of some sudden developments in the market is futuristic and is part of managing the future. It is rather critical that attention be paid to both. As we defined them, symptoms and indicators both need to be examined. But, quite often, firms are so preoccupied with their present performances that they cannot see beyond them. Such incumbent behavior is very common. But here the futuristic attitude based on assessing and reacting to indicators is more counterchaotic than examining our performance through symptoms within the constraints of our incumbent attitude. In the case of symptoms, we can have corrective action but this does not improve or enhance our capability to cope with an event that causes chaotic waves. As long as the difference between the two, that is, symptoms and indicators, is understood, we need both. One would lead to corrective action, and the other one to counterchaos strategies. Thus, performance assessment (symptoms) is critical, but market assessment (indicators) is even more important to assess the firm's performance and keep it objective by weighing it against dramatic and unexpected developments in the marketplace.

PERFORMANCE ASSESSMENT

All companies have goals, strategic plans, and plans of action or implementation. Many would also add a component to the process, which may be coined a performance assessment, an early indicator, a feedback, or some other word. The critical point here is that early performance assessment is key, but it must be weighed against possible and unexpected future changes in the market.

Assume, for instance, you are the leader of a company. You have a vision. You have a strong managerial team, and you have carefully selected and trained human resources. The corporate culture that you have developed is in place, helping to achieve corporate goals. While everything is moving smoothly, suddenly, and most unexpectedly, a competitor emerges and changes the total makeup of your market like a bolt of lightening. What have you done so far to detect, cope, and react to such a situation? If your market is very dynamic, you expect that this chaotic shock is not the only one you would experience. The question is what kind of provisions, if any, did you make in your strategic plans for such situations?[1]

INDICATORS VERSUS SYMPTOMS

Performance assessment procedure can be seen in Figure 4.1. Typical marketing inputs such as product, promotion, place, and price (known as the 4 Ps) are all in place. Here strategic planning is influenced by the external uncontrollables that would vary from unexpected competition to a serious business slowdown. As the strategic plan implementation, modified by external uncontrollables, takes place, early symptoms start appearing. Early symptoms of our performance indicating how well we are doing certainly can be connected to or influenced by the environmental

Figure 4.1.
Performance Assessment.

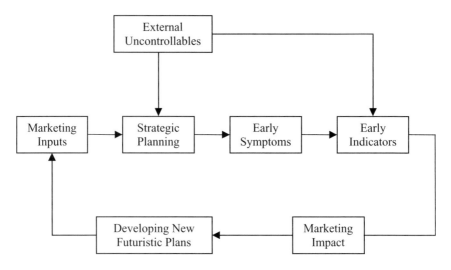

or uncontrollable and unexpected sudden developments revealed by these early indicators. Here, the marketing impact is the expected combination of symptoms and indicators. The marketing impact might reveal the need for a different marketing plan that is more futuristic on the basis of the performance assessment activity. It must be dramatically emphasized that the total process presented in Figure 4.1 is a circular, ongoing activity. It never stops and, if done properly, it raises the performance level of the company and makes the company reasonably chaos-resistant. One key aspect of Figure 4.1 is the time dimension. If the symptoms and indicators point in the direction of a new strategic plan, that plan must be prepared and implemented extremely swiftly.

In Figure 4.1, symptoms and indicators are separated. In Table 4.1, a special attempt is made to illustrate these two. However, it is also clear that they are reasonably and seriously connected. Perhaps if the company were to pay more attention to indicators, it would not experience some of the symptoms indicating a major ailment or ailments in its performance. There is a question as to what Kodak's executives thought when the symptoms indicated a very significant decline in their business. If they attributed the decline to the quality of their products and their marketing practices, they were certainly facing chaos. If indicators earlier pointed out that digital photography was gaining tremendous momentum, executives might have been prepared to have a totally different product line and other counterchaos measures.

Table 4.1
Early Performance Evaluation Criteria Examples

Symptoms	Indicators
• Our newly introduced product was immediately sold out.	Certain demand-stimulating factors indicate that this product will be very successful.
• An unusual level of product returns and requests for parts occurs.	There are indicators showing that there are better versions of the product by competitors; consumer values are changing.
• Our stars and cash cows have become dogs.	There are serious indicators dealing with a dramatic change in the preferences and needs of consumers.
• Our cost-based low price products are taking a major beating.	There is evidence for a significant boom in the economy; consumers need better service than simply low prices.
• Our snack food introduction is a complete bust.	Evidence indicates a very strong move toward healthy snacks.

ENTER CHAOS THEORY

Although chaos theory has been primarily explored in conjunction with physics, mathematics, and biology, it is also becoming increasingly important in social sciences as well. Chaos theory (CT), however, has not been utilized much in relationship to business strategies and marketing activity. Parts of this theory are important enough to provide important insight particularly in extremely dynamic markets. Some of the general premises of the theory are utilized as part of the counterchaos marketing strategy that is presented in this book.

What Is Chaos Theory?

As discussed in Chapter 1, chaos theorists do not quite agree on the specifics of the theory. While some theorists think that chaos is orderly disorder, others believe that it is punctuated equilibrium. Yet others consider it to be the change theory or nonlinear dynamics. From a mathematical perspective, chaos theory attempts to understand the pattern and structures behind nonlinear systems. If there is such divergence in thinking, how can a counterchaos theory be articulated for marketing decision-makers? The present author believes that, from a marketing perspective, chaos can be detected, but it is not likely to repeat itself in an orderly manner. Its impact can hardly be totally assessed in advance, it does not fit into a pattern, and it does not have a detectable structure. And, above all, it comes very unexpectedly with tremendous destructive vigor. In other words, chaos is not orderly disorder but *disorderly disorder*.[2]

In the 1960s, Edward Lorenz[3] developed a theory indicating that "if a butterfly flaps its wings in Asia it causes a hurricane in the Atlantic." In other words, small changes or events create complex and unexpected consequences at a broader level in the future.[4] This is where this author parts company with chaos theory. First, there is no reason to assume that a small event "A" will always generate a big impact "B." In different markets, "A" may cause totally different results, such as the Asian financial crisis in 1998. The nature of that crisis and its impact were all different in different countries. Second, in the marketplace, the time span is totally unpredictable. In one market event "A" may cause a dramatic change of "B" in the market after 5 years, while in another market, "A" may create a dramatic change of "C" immediately. The emphasis on chaos as being disorderly disorder thus is reinforced. Indeed, there may be order in chaos in the long run, but our company will not live that long to see and/or benefit from that order. Therefore, chaos must be detected and reacted to immediately. Consequently, it has to be treated in the very short run as disorderly disorder.

CONVERTING CHAOS INTO OPPORTUNITY

Proactive counterchaos orientation implies converting chaotic market events into opportunities. In order to accomplish this, some chaos theorists maintain that companies must become *complex adaptive systems*.[5] Here the word "adaptive" is questioned. The corporate entity must be at the cutting edge of the chaotic market development and adapt to it, not only to survive, but also to be able to use it to benefit itself. Figure 4.2 illustrates how chaotic market developments can become opportunities: First, the overall approach of the company is not to solve problems but to capitalize on new opportunities. Thus, the company must always be focused on market developments and the company's capabilities. Second, all the events and information in and about the market must be immediately handled by commensurate policies and procedures. Third, considering each and every change and development in the market as a new opportunity is essential for the opportunistic outlook. Finally, developing new products

Figure 4.2.
Opportunistic Outlook.

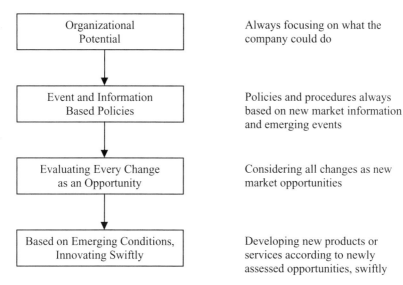

Organizational Potential	Always focusing on what the company could do
Event and Information Based Policies	Policies and procedures always based on new market information and emerging events
Evaluating Every Change as an Opportunity	Considering all changes as new market opportunities
Based on Emerging Conditions, Innovating Swiftly	Developing new products or services according to newly assessed opportunities, swiftly

and/or new services commensurate to the changes and developments in the market swiftly and effectively is the delivery of the opportunistic system's approach. A company such as Perkin-Elmer Applied Biosystems can be an example. The Perkin-Elmer Corporation is the world leader in the development, manufacturing, and marketing of the science systems and analytical instrumentation used in markets such as biotechnology and others. Not only has the company shown a nearly 20 percent annual growth for the past two decades or so, but also, every year, 50 to 65 percent of its sales are generated by products that did not even exist a year ago. It appears that developing such an opportunistic outlook is keeping the company at the cutting edge of the industry. In order to develop such an outlook, typically it is necessary to develop and use an opportunity budgeting system.

OPPORTUNITY BUDGETING

A proactive counterchaos orientation is necessary to counteract the unexpected and powerful adversities in the marketplace. Here the firm not only looks at early indicators and symptoms but also moves quickly to convert the changes in the market to opportunities. The firm must be committed to organized, continuous, and disciplined effort to maintain its opportunistic outlook. This implies that the firm commits some of its resources to actual and potential results as the changing and emerging opportunities are used to best advantage. Drucker,[6] in conjunction with this type of thinking, proposed a new concept, which he coined as opportunity budgeting.

In his words, "One way to exercise assignment control and to concentrate is to have two budgets, an operational budget for the things that are already being done and an opportunities budget for the proposed new and different ventures." He goes on to say that "for the opportunities budget, the first question is: 'Is this the right opportunity for us?' And if the answer is 'yes' one asks: 'What is the optimum efforts and resources this opportunity can absorb and put to productive use?'" Finally, he says that "the opportunities budget should be optimized, that is, funded to give the highest rate of return for efforts and expenditures."

Thus, the opportunity budget is a proactive budget that supports the firm's opportunistic outlook. It is based on the most suitable and promising market opportunities that the firm is experiencing. Obviously the most important point in the development of such a budget is the identification and prioritization of the changing and newly emerging opportunities. A process to accomplish this goal is presented in this section. It must be reiterated that the opportunity budgeting process is primarily based on the firm's opportunistic outlook (Figure 4.2).

ZEROING IN ON THE OPPORTUNITIES

The more opportunistic the firm is, the greater its survival capability in the face of chaotic market changes. Figure 4.3 illustrates a five-stage-development leading to successful construction of an opportunity budget. The stages are specified from very general external to most specific internal.

The first stage is identifying opportunities: measuring markets, their growth rate, and their need changes and other chaotic influences that can be extremely important potential opportunities for the firm. It is critical to assess these and convert them into products or services and approximate their respective sales volume.

Once the opportunities are identified, they need to be scaled down on the basis of the threats. These threats stem primarily from increased competition or deteriorating market conditions. What if, for instance, the identified opportunities are rather temporary or some other firm has better skills to take advantage of this opportunity?

The next step is to analyze the firm's own capabilities. Its strengths must be such that it could take advantage of the external market opportunities

Figure 4.3.
Zeroing-In on the Opportunities.

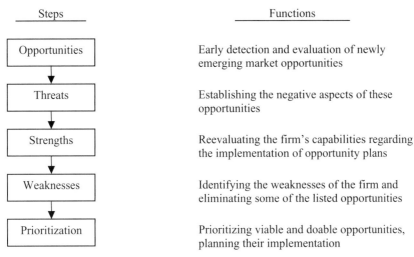

Steps	Functions
Opportunities	Early detection and evaluation of newly emerging market opportunities
Threats	Establishing the negative aspects of these opportunities
Strengths	Reevaluating the firm's capabilities regarding the implementation of opportunity plans
Weaknesses	Identifying the weaknesses of the firm and eliminating some of the listed opportunities
Prioritization	Prioritizing viable and doable opportunities, planning their implementation

Source: Adapted and revised from Samli (1993).

or sudden changes. This means translating market opportunities into the firm's resources and capabilities.

All firms have certain weaknesses. It is critical to scale down the firm's strengths against its weaknesses. Even though the newly detected market opportunities may be especially attractive, if capitalizing on these implies not eliminating the firm's weaknesses and not using its strengths, then it is quite likely that those opportunities may not have a high priority in the firm's marketing plans.

Finally, the fifth step is prioritization. Once a number of newly emerging opportunities are isolated and scaled down, some of them are likely to be most attractive as opposed to others. It is, therefore, extremely important to prioritize opportunities from most to least attractive. Figure 4.3, as can be seen, provides the essentials of the opportunity budget.[7]

DEVELOPING THE OPPORTUNITY BUDGET

The effectiveness of the opportunity budget, first and foremost, depends on the firm's capability of prioritizing its newly emerging and market indicated opportunities. If the first phase of the process, that is zeroing in on the opportunities, is not done properly and effectively, the results could be detrimental.

As stated by Samli,[8] the opportunity budget determines the future survival of the company and should be optimized so that the firm's probabilities for success in the near future are also optimized. This means while the funding for different opportunities should be commensurate with their priority ordering, there should also be ample resources allocated to unforeseen opportunities as well as to drastic and unexpected changes in the prioritization of the ranking of these opportunities. It is apparent that the whole opportunity budgeting process needs to be extremely flexible and forward-looking so that the firm can cope with unexpected and chaotic changes in the marketplace and convert them into opportunities.

COUNTERCHAOS MARKETING

Performance assessment, indicators, and symptoms, all are outreach efforts of the company. It is critical that the firm manage its future by detecting, understanding, and evaluating the chaotic shock waves. *Counterchaos marketing is successfully detecting important developments in the market and converting them into profitable ventures.* This will require not only a major change in the organization from being reactive to becoming proactive, but also a major *paradigm shift.* The company's understanding of what it does and where it is headed is most likely to change so that it will be managing market adversities as an opportunity. In other words, counterchaos marketing is ultimately proactive behavior. Some of the details of that behavior are discussed in the next chapter. However, it is critical to reiterate that this paradigm shift, represented by the ultimate in proactive behavior, stands for a new way of managing.

Drucker[9] stated that managers in the 21st century are not going to order around their subordinates. Instead, the team will make the decisions and run the company. Companies such as Motorola and 3M have been, at least partially, using such an orientation by allowing everybody in the organization to participate in the process of innovating new products and services.

A basic question in developing new products and new services still remains. Diversion versus conversion is likely to be used in the development of products and industries. Diversion means developing a concept or a product completely independently without referring to other products and past experiences. Conversion implies bringing two known technologies together to generate a new one. Which of these is more critical to emphasize? When Casio developed wristwatches with digital cameras, this was an instance of convergence of two different industries and technologies.

So was, for instance, the electric typewriter. It appears that many products are developed by convergence. However, most of the key industries and products that emerged during the past half a century or so are perhaps based on divergence. PCs, for example, are not convergence of hand calculators and electricity. Televisions did not come about by converging radios and photography. Current efforts to develop numerous revolutionary products by Hewlett Packard are all based on divergence. Although somewhat profitable, convergence-based products, here, are considered to be reactive and rather short-lived, whereas divergence-based products are proactive and more powerful in the long run. This distinction between divergence and convergence and the future implications of both types of developments must be researched more thoroughly.

COUNTERACTING CRITICAL CHANGES

One of the key points posited here is that when critical changes are emerging in the market, for instance, an economic recession is becoming noticeable, counteracting such a development, unlike common thinking, is not a matter of cost-cutting, laying off workers, or moving the factories from one country to another. A market development must be counteracted with marketing activities. Improving promotion, putting more emphasis on services, and introducing new products are all part of such a marketing reaction. Thus, counterrecession marketing becomes a form of trendsetting, which, if done carefully, can be a most powerful marketing activity toward improving the firm's market position.

CRITICAL COUNTERCHAOS CHECKLIST

1. Are we carefully and objectively assessing our performance?
2. Are we contrasting market indicators and performance-related symptoms?
3. What do we know about the chaos theory that may influence us?
4. Can we convert chaotic changes in the marketplace into new opportunities?
5. Do we have enough financial flexibility to emphasize new market opportunities?

SUMMARY

All firms need to develop a performance assessment system. Such a system will be composed of indicators and symptoms and will enable the firm to detect chaotic influences early in the market.

Chaos theory has not found itself in marketing literature and practice. Unlike typical chaos theory orientation, it is posited in this chapter that chaos is disorderly disorder. Hence, it is critical to detect it early and counteract it effectively. Chaos, if detected early, can be converted to opportunity. Proactive marketing can maintain an opportunistic outlook with the support of an opportunity budget, such that proactivity generates resistance to chaotic developments and develops market power.

Chapter 5

The Role of the Counterchaos Marketer

If the marketing manager wants to manage the future by trendsetting, a number of tasks need to be performed. Performance of these tasks would not only enhance the chances for survival but also convert chaotic developments in the marketplace into opportunities. This all means developing a resilient group of people to absorb *future shocks*. The employees of the company need to be taught the characteristics that are needed to become a more resilient company in times of dramatic change or chaos. Thomson Corporation of Stamford, Connecticut, has developed courses to this end. The human resources of the company are taught to be focused, organized, proactive, and to have a positive sense of ability to deal with or change chaos.[1]

THE ROLE OF THE MANAGER AND MARKETING ACTION

The role of the manager and the marketing actions to be followed are presented in Table 5.1. Eleven specific areas are identified in the exhibit, which are discussed below. It must be stated at the outset that this is not an exhaustive list, but it is an important one.

Much of the thinking here comes from chaos theory that defies accepted ways of thinking and reasoning. In other words, where chaos begins, conventional and classical ways of thinking stops because chaos theory poses ways that defy accepted ways of solving problems. Since this theory can be generally defined as the study of complex systems that are

Table 5.1
Counterchaos Marketing Practices

The Role of the Marketing Manager	Marketing Action
• Manage the transition	Always be ready to enter different markets or generate different products.
• Build resilience	Reduce the action time to implement strategic alternatives or contingency plans.
• Destabilize the system	Change the inflexible policies and procedures and perform the unexpected if necessary.
• Manage order and disorder	Convert chaos-causing unexpected events into new opportunities systematically.
• Create and maintain a learning organization	Establish and implement a Strategic Information System (SIS) based on data converted into information and implementation.
• Utilize bifurcation as a tool	Be capable of choosing from opposite and contradictory alternatives
• Find the ways to promote renewal	Always be able to find new ways of improving market position.
• Manage carefully transformation	Develop the ability to do whatever it takes to cope with chaotic changes in the marketplace.
• Pay special attention to disruptive technologies	Keep your technical antennae up and invest aggressively in new technologies.
• Explore carefully latent demands of consumers	By using indicators and logic develop a system that would evaluate latent demand.
• Be ready for sudden and unexpected economic recession	A counterrecession marketing activity dealing with more promotion, more aggressive marketing, or a possible change in the merchandise mix.

Source: Adapted and revised from Samli.[2]

constantly changing, the thinking and orientation that it brings to the business decision-making arena is suitable for coping with ever-changing markets and competitive postures. If chaos is order without predictability, as some describe it, businesses will have to manage it with similar unpredictability, implying that counterchaos activities and decisions cannot come from linear thinking and reasoning. Unexpected developments in the market, economy, and competition must be dealt with in ways that would not at all make sense in the framework of conventional wisdom. Since the amount and intensity of disorder or chaos has continued to increase, the 11 specific action areas identified in Table 5.1 must be taken very seriously. These are all options in implementing a counterchaos strategy for survival and success in everchanging and increasingly unfriendly markets.

MANAGING TRANSITION

Managing transitions implies being ready to enter different markets, generate different products, or change major corporate policies on a very short notice. It may mean cutting certain product or service life cycles unexpectedly short. IBM made such a transition as it switched from mainframes to personal computers. Here, however, managing this dramatic change smoothly and swiftly becomes a critical concern. In describing how Intel faced a major defect in its microprocessor chip inside the computer, Grove[3] states that "We all need to expose ourselves to the winds of change." As a result, the company changed its replacement policy completely and satisfied the needs of 25,000 computer users daily, who were calling and requesting a new part.

BUILDING RESILIENCE

Building resilience for the company implies versatility to a point of reducing the reaction time when dramatic action is required to make major changes in the strategic posture of the firm due to unexpected shock waves. When Wal-Mart superstores entered small communities, some stores quickly became category killers to survive the shock. Home Depot and Toys R Us have been aggressively following policies of a low price and great variety, policies to counteract the increasing unfriendliness of the market.

DESTABILIZING THE SYSTEM

Many companies, in time, develop rather inflexible policies and procedures. Destabilizing would mean changing these policies and procedures rather swiftly and performing the unexpected, if necessary. This may mean anything from suddenly changing the company strategic business units (SBUs) to completely changing the company's target market. To survive, Sears had to destabilize its system by eliminating its very vast financial activities.

MANAGING DISORDER

Managing disorder is detecting an impact out of chaos. From a marketing perspective, this means converting chaos-causing dramatic events into new opportunities that the firm can take advantage of. As elaborated in Chapter 4, there are major new opportunities behind the chaotic events. Thus the firm can routinely learn to convert these events into action programs. Intel moved from being a producer of computer chips to becoming a manufacturer of microprocessors.[4] A computer firm may have to explore nanotechnologies before these technologies make the company's products totally obsolete.

DEVELOPING AND MAINTAINING A LEARNING ORGANIZATION

Developing and maintaining a learning organization indicates how well the firm is equipped to generate critical information for its decision-making activity. All organizations learn as they survive. This topic is explored in greater detail in Chapter 6. Suffice it to say here that learning organizations don't just wait to survive and hence generate information. They are rather proactive. Such learning organizations proactively search, generate, and disseminate information for critical decision areas. Some scholars maintain that if innovations were to be adopted successfully by an organization, these innovations must be complementary to other supporting innovations so that the larger system can be reintegrated. In order to accomplish this, new information technologies will be placed in the organization. In other words, the organization must become a learning organization in order for technologies and organizational structures to coexist, evolve, and reach higher plateaus. Many interconnected computer networks can generate and disseminate much data for managers everywhere. Here the learning organization is particularly preoccupied with learning how to identify forthcoming storms in the market and how to react to them quickly.

UTILIZE BIFURCATION AS A TOOL

Bifurcation can be considered a tool of counterchaos culture in the sense that in order to cope with chaos, sometimes extreme and totally opposing decision alternatives, to current ones, need to be considered. Companies, because of a particular chaotic development in the marketplace, may face a situation of abandoning the whole product line or replacing it with the least expected group of products. The Internet, for instance, can easily take over the traditional telecommunications industry or can just have a shocking impact on the software industry. It can create much different software packages and distribute them effectively. Similarly, automobiles operated by fuel cells may take over the traditional automotive industry. Such a shock can easily cause bifurcation on the part of traditional auto manufacturers as they modify their whole operations to survive.

FIND THE WAYS TO PROMOTE RENEWAL

Creating an orientation and atmosphere of renewal among individuals, teams, the whole organization, and its presence in the marketplace is essential for the corporation to counteract shock waves. Spirited resurgence of the firm in the marketplace cannot be left to luck or to sheer accident. The firm must be fully prepared to renew its strengths, its products and services, its intellectual capital and, above all, its competitive advantage in the presence of chaotic conditions. Only a few of the old vertical computer companies survived in the newly emerged horizontal computer industry. The others could not create an atmosphere of renewal to adapt themselves to a completely new and different industry structure.[5]

MANAGE TRANSFORMATION

The changing conditions can be so dramatic that the firm may need a complete transformation. This may require a large variety of new alternatives to become a part of the immediate choice decisions that the firm is facing immediately. The choices may include alternatives such as a complete change of target markets, a complete change in product lines, moving in the direction of the firm from being a manufacturer to becoming a total importer, or closing the manufacturing plants and moving out of the country. Transforming the company into something totally different from what it is certainly calls for a different state of mind and different preparation procedures.

PAY SPECIAL ATTENTION TO DISRUPTIVE TECHNOLOGIES

Disruptive technologies are a major source of chaos. As digital photography, mobile telephones, hand-held digital appliances, and the like emerge, the established technologies may need to do something dramatic. Disruptive technologies, as opposed to established technologies, move fast. They are cheaper, they produce better or different products, and they primarily impact the best companies that do not feel an immediate need to change. Slow moving, well-established companies in fast-moving industries and dynamic markets become extremely vulnerable. In the long run, these disruptive technologies become mainstream and, in turn, they may become vulnerable to new and emerging disruptive technologies.[6] As disruptive technologies emerge, they send shock waves to current and traditional industries.

EXPLORE LATENT DEMANDS

Latent demands of consumers are perhaps the most important sources of sudden chaotic influences. For example, when consumers were confronted with the availability of power tools, significant shock waves went through the traditional tool manufacturers. Up until the late 1970s, there was no such thing as aerobics. But suddenly high-impact, low-impact, no-impact aerobics emerged, each with its own equipment, wardrobes, and other supplies. This almost completely changed exercise and fitness programs. By using indicators, symptoms, and, above all, logic, the firm can develop a system that will first indicate and then evaluate latent demands. It is particularly important to realize that latent demands for one generation are strictly old-fashioned for the next. The firm must always be futuristic and proactive.[7]

SUDDEN AND UNEXPECTED ECONOMIC RECESSION

Economic recessions are not uncommon in our economy. They appear unexpectedly and send shock waves to more vulnerable businesses in more sensitive sectors in our economy. Counterchaos marketing proposes a proactive posture. The firms, instead of cutting down costs and contracting their outreach, must initiate a counterattack. For instance, companies that, during the recession, did not cut down their advertising activity but, in fact, increased it selectively and wisely have done better than their counterparts that took drastic measures to cut down their costs and expenses. Part of the counterchaos activity could easily be a major change in the company's product mix. Inland Motors located in the southwestern part of Virginia responded to the 1982 recession by developing more cost, fuel, and price-efficient motors and stopped their more expensive models. This,

Figure 5.1.
Impact of Counterchaos Behavior

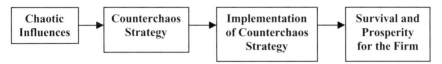

at the time, worked like a charm. The company maintained its status and was not negatively affected by the recession.

THE COUNTERCHAOS MARKETER REVISITED

The list presented in this chapter and particularly in Table 5.1, indicating the role of the counterchaos marketing manager can easily be expanded. There are perhaps numerous other key roles the proactive marketing manager needs to play. However, it is critical to realize that none of the roles attributed to the counterchaos marketing manager can be identified as "business as usual." Just what would it take to expect the unexpected and adjust to that unexpected event becoming a reality? Certainly thinking out of the box and indeed, as discussed in Chapter 1, even changing the box are necessary ingredients of counterchaos marketing. Particularly, converting the chaotic influence into an important opportunity presents the crux of thinking that is presented throughout this book. Just how such an orientation can be instilled into the thinking of a decision-maker still remains a mystery that needs to be explored forcefully. This is the future of successful managerial action.

THE OVERALL IMPACT

The 11 separate roles attributed to management in the implementation of a general counterchaos strategy, may be used one at a time, a number of them can be used simultaneously, or all of them can be implemented at the same time. All in all, the impact of the counterchaos strategy, if implemented successfully, is a tremendous benefit for the firm. Figure 5.1 illustrates the sequence of events in this general orientation.

Even if one is used separately and exclusively, the 11 separate roles of marketing managers, to fight off chaos, may somewhat overlap. But they may also indicate different alternatives that may be effective for different industries and firms under different circumstances. It must be reiterated that chaos-creating forces do not have equal and detectable impact in all industries and in all firms. Thus, each situation must be evaluated according to its own merits.

The Fate of the Fashion Center

The Fashion Center (a retail establishment of apparel) had been located in the same place for the past 40 years or so. While it was located in the most prestigious section of a large midwestern city, the location deteriorated as modern suburbs and shopping centers emerged. While it was a popular store of primarily male apparel and certainly had a lot to say about the most recent fashions, the store and its location had lost their charm and their reputation. The management had to decide that the retail establishment's future is not at all the continuation of the past. There was a need for a dramatic change and breaking away from the past. The management explored and established a retail establishment dealing with uniforms of all types. After so many years in existence, The Fashion Center became the uniform center of the city. It promoted itself aggressively and proved that consumer value can be established in different ways. Simultaneously, the company established its own counterchaos measure.

CRITICAL COUNTERCHAOS CHECKLIST

1. Do we have the type of management that can successfully cope with the chaotic conditions in the market?
2. Can we possibly make a total change in our practices to cope with market changes?
3. What are the key elements of the necessary changes in our practices?
4. Can we prioritize the necessary changes that may be expected of us?
5. Can we evaluate the impact of the implemented counterchaos strategies quickly?

SUMMARY

The marketing manager, who is managing his/her company's future and seeking opportunities to raise the company's performance level in the marketplace to higher plateaus, must play multiple roles and perform various marketing actions. Eleven such roles and related marketing actions are identified in this chapter. All of these are proactive and futuristic. The counterchaos marketing manager, by definition, must think out of the box.

The 11 roles are: managing the transition, building resilience, destabilizing the system, managing disorder, creating a learning organization, utilizing bifurcation, finding ways to promote renewal, managing transformation, paying attention to disruptive technologies, exploring latent demand, and being ready for economic recessions. Perhaps the key reminder here is that an action-filled strategy is required and **wishful** thinking is not one.

Chapter 6

Developing a Learning Organization

The corporate culture, the power, and the value system that overlooks and directs all of the company activities, requires or revolves around four key areas: inspiration, reward, atmosphere, and values.[1] The corporate work environment must inspire all to do their best. Of course, doing their best on the part of everybody implies the presence of a proper reward system that is sensitive to performance and accomplishments. The atmosphere of work must be so that individuals are not only challenged and satisfied but also having fun. Finally, establishing clear corporate values and abiding by them is a necessary part of the total culture. Not only the development of such a culture but also its sustainability depends on if there is a learning organization that is carrying out the corporate culture, revising when it needs to be revised, and providing the information to manage the viability of the corporate culture. Companies such as Microsoft, Home Depot, and Walgreen's are very sensitive to the need and management of information to implement the proper corporate culture. These companies use acquired knowledge to determine how their customers are best served, what additional functions may be required, and where in the organization to improve the overall performance. Although this is a solid approach to managing the present, it is not enough to manage the future well unless the learning organization orientation is taken to the front burner. In fact, much of the time, companies are so extremely busy managing the present that they forget to manage the future. Here the learning organization concept plays a critical role.

Since chaos acts like a tornado and since it is destructive but also potentially very lucrative, it is critical that the firm be capable of responding

Figure 6.1.
Counterchaos Learning Process.

proactively. Discontinuous and disorderly market forces causing chaotic situations need to be encountered with equally discontinuous and equally disorderly innovations or marketing practices that represent paradigm shifts. Here the effectiveness and speed of paradigm shifts are critical. Early and accurate detection of the market facts and the profundity of the proposed paradigm shift will be the key determinants of the firm's counterchaos strategy. Such a strategy, above all, depends on how the firm receives and manages information.

As early as 1982, John Naisbitt[2] stated that the American society was in transition. It was moving from being an industrial society to an information society. Peter Drucker[3] dwelled upon the emergence and the importance of information workers. He reiterated what Naisbitt posited, the American society is still in transition and is becoming more and more entrenched with information generation and use. With the development of the Internet and information technology, the amounts of data available for businesses are almost incomprehensible. However, this is not what is commonly coined information overload but, rather, it is data overload that businesses are suffering from.[4] If the data are not processed, organized, and analyzed appropriately, they do not become information useful to the decision maker. But, generating information is not enough. Business must learn by absorbing and using that information. In the proactive marketing orientation where the business is inventing and managing the future, information is extremely critical, and it will not be available and useable if the learning process is not taking place.

In order for learning to take place, there must be information. If the firm does not have the capability to generate critical data and convert them into information, there cannot be any learning in the organization. Without any possibility of learning, the firm cannot possibly survive the chaotic shock waves emanating from the market. Figure 6.1 illustrates the relationship between the chaotic market influences and the development of counterchaos strategies. It must be reiterated that the nature of the data gathered modifies the nature of the information generated and, once again, without information, there is no learning.

Figure 6.2.
Development of A Strategic Information System.

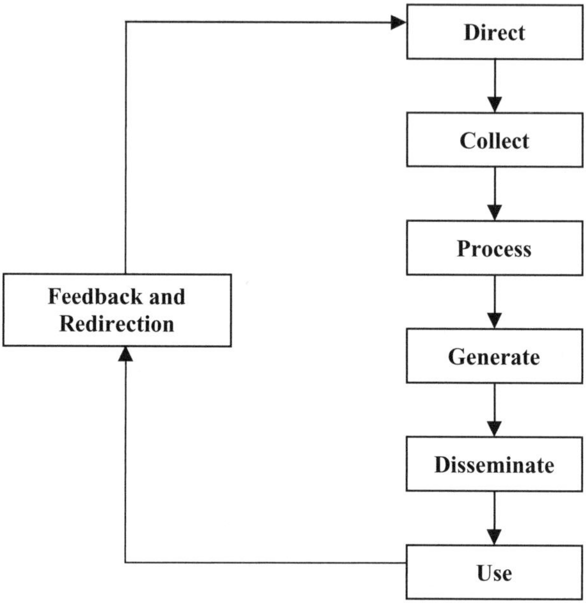

Source: Adapted and revised from Samli (1996).

FROM DATA TO STRATEGIC DECISIONS

All firms must have a strategic information system (SIS). The development of an SIS has six key steps. Figure 6.2 illustrates these steps. Without the sequential order of these steps, data cannot become information, and information does not become a strategy. Of course, as the strategy is implemented, learning also takes place so that strategic plans are revised as needed. Thus, after the feedback the redirection activities are put to use as learning would indicate.[5]

Although the six steps presented in Figure 6.2 are reasonably self-explanatory, a brief discussion is presented. Directing the firm's research activity, as to what needs to be researched and who's in charge, is the starting point (step one). How data should be gathered and from which sources is a critical second step. Step three is the critical point where data are converted into information. Critical information bases are generated in the fourth step. The information that is generated is disseminated in step five. Finally, the information that is made available is used to develop and implement marketing strategies (step six). Feedback and redirection activity is a necessary component of the whole process. Without an SIS such as the one presented here, there cannot be a counterchaos strategy.

A DICHOTOMY OF LEARNING

Although all organizations learn as they survive and succeed, such learning is primarily an extension of the conventional wisdom discussed in Chapter 3 of this book. By definition, a firm surviving in the marketplace is learning, but this type of learning is reactive and does not necessarily put the firm in an advantageous competitive position. This is not the type of learning those who are coined learning organizations are engaged in. Learning organizations, unlike standard organizational learning, generate and manage their information and integrate that information into their management systems proactively and selectively. A learning organization is skilled at creating, acquiring, and transferring knowledge, as well as modifying its behavior and its strategies to generate new knowledge and new insights. Perhaps, above all, it is using the newly acquired information to modify its behavior quickly and effectively. This means the learning in this organization is institutionalized and used proactively by being integrated into the firm's management systems.

Even though there is an emerging multibillion dollar knowledge management market, there is not enough evidence that there is a unique and accelerating learning activity. The knowledge management does not even make the distinction between organizational learning and learning organization and that learning organizations are prone to perform better in the marketplace due to their fast and proper learning activity. Thus, it is necessary for organizations to examine their learning capabilities as part of their strategic posture for success.

THE KNOWLEDGE CHAIN

Although there is a rich literature available on knowledge management, which is related to organizational learning, this literature does not identify the key characteristics of a *learning organization*. However, it is reiterated here that if the organization does not learn as part of its strategic focus and does not use this knowledge proactively, the value of information and the value of what has been learned are almost nullified or at least overlooked or ignored. The more the organization is prone to learning proactively, the greater its market performance. Here, the knowledge chain is instilled in the organization's activities so that any managerial decision will benefit from the constantly incoming information.

As data are gathered, converted into information, and implemented in the form of strategies, knowledge accumulates. Here is where the critical point lies. The generated knowledge within the organization must not be lost and, above all, must be involved in critical decision situations. For instance, advertising knowledge must be adequate to make sound advertising decisions, and the pricing knowledge should lead to better pricing decisions. The rest of the marketing decisions, again, are based on marketing knowledge that is generated and made available wherever and whenever it is needed. Thus, learning organizations develop *knowledge chains*, which generate knowledge and make it available when and where it is needed. In order to set up an adequate knowledge chain, certain key factors need to be present. Ten such key factors discussed below.[6]

KEY FACTORS OF THE KNOWLEDGE CHAIN

Although most companies might think of themselves as learning organizations, it is quite doubtful that they are capable of distinguishing between organizational learning and learning organizations or maybe, more specifically, between passive versus proactive learning. Without this distinction, these organizations cannot improve their own learning capabilities. In order to distinguish between passive and proactive learning, 10 key factors are identified here. In order for an organization to be a learning organization, it must excel in all of these 10 factors. These are specified and discussed below.

Organizational Leadership

An organization's leaders need to actively support the premise of a learning organization. All corporate cultures take on the personality of their leaders and their style. It is a common belief that top management has great influence over those within the organization regarding the creation of a general knowledge structure. An open and sharing style will encourage individual knowledge and wisdom sharing through multiple media. On the other hand, the building of corporate wisdom will require time and capital commitments with results that are difficult to measure. If top management does not consider knowledge development as a strategic activity, there will be no success in this direction. The leaders will expect to be the beneficiaries of corporate wisdom during the decision-making process. The idea here is for the leaders to recognize that they need to create and sustain momentum so that contributions to corporate wisdom are not a unique experience, but a routine and daily event.

Internal Communication

Internal communication has a direct effect on corporate learning or the lack thereof. If an organization does not encourage communication and knowledge-sharing within itself, then organizational learning will be concentrated in the hands of a few individuals who may or may not share the already accumulated information with those critical people who need this information for effective decision-making. Thus, the organizational learning process becomes stagnant and lopsided. Here, of course, the key is not collecting more and more knowledge by "higher-ups." Rather, it is finding more and more ways of getting connected with the people at the firing line so that the knowledge can be interrelated. The typical current practice is that communication is encouraged at local levels among individuals and small groups, and not at the higher organizational level and among large groups. However, this situation can be and, in fact, should be rectified by utilizing informal procedures such as coffee room discussions and other types of discussion sessions along with formal procedures such as reports, site visits, personnel rotation programs, and others. Of course, the more formal and far-reaching communication systems are being developed through the most up-to-date information technology advancements.

Type of Resources

This organized attribute in many ways is a result of the type of business the company is in. It may employ individuals who are focused in their work and ignore extraneous activities such as sharing knowledge. Many service organizations employ those who are the product creators and therefore are accustomed to sharing knowledge with the customer. Here the critical point is to convince those employees that sharing knowledge internally will ultimately benefit the customer, which in turn would add value to the company as a whole and would enhance its market power. Companies are now hiring those who have a balance of intelligence and the ability to communicate and work with others. This goes against the conventional wisdom and conventional practice of hiring the most intelligent people we can find and not worrying if they are interacting with the outside world.

Amount of Quality Research

As stated earlier, without research there cannot be any information and, without information, there is no learning. Thus, how much research is undertaken, how much information is generated, and how successfully this information is shared by the whole organization are all critical activities of a learning organization. Generating quality research and distributing its results in the form of knowledge throughout the organization can be a critical challenge. The majority of the people in the organization may not have the same capacity to receive and digest research-generated information. Therefore, some part of the information may be ignored or bypassed. Learning organizations must make a concerted effort to generate, communicate, and use research-based knowledge both internally and externally.

Mobility of the Corporate Culture

In addition to the prevailing unusually high-level workforce mobility, current merger mania that is rampant in the American economy and hostile takeovers are creating further mobility. Workforce mobility partially or fully disrupts organizational learning. Knowledge that is needed by the organization is held by individuals who leave the firm. The lower the average tenure of people in the organization, the more difficult it becomes to maintain a corporate culture of continuous learning. Often those who leave the company depart with individual knowledge and wisdom that was never transferred to others. Unless serious effort is made to keep knowledge in the organization, this situation causes the organization to lose learning capacity. This is a very costly proposition, since the new recruits have to learn everything from scratch and there is no accumulated knowledge in the organization.

Degree of Interaction among Corporate Offices

As the virtual office permeates corporate cultures, the amount of interaction among the staff decreases. If interaction among individual employees is reduced, so is the sharing of information, knowledge, and experiences. Typically decentralized organizations do not have the networking capabilities to keep the parts of the organization connected. They are also susceptible to fragmented learning, wherein some part of the organization may be learning much more than others. Consulting organizations are particularly plagued by such problems. Most of their work is project-based, which keeps the workforce mobile and rarely in a proper corporate environment where fellow employees stay and work together for an extended period of time. Such situations make it difficult to enhance organizational learning. There needs to be a greater reliance on technology to increase communication within the organization and disseminate information adequately among employees. Knowledge databases are becoming popular in consulting organizations. This gives those mobile employees a central source of information to access and to expand.

Technical Architecture

This factor determines the ease or difficulty of adding to and receiving corporate wisdom. The architecture is often seen as the first step in the organizational knowledge development process. Typically, first the organization puts an information technology infrastructure in place and then goes beyond the technology to view the management of information itself as a major asset to generate competitive advantage. The knowledge database is the term most often used to define the central repository for corporate knowledge. The traditional approach has been to use data-intensive computer terminals and reports. A transition is being made to more textual-based alternatives in terms of providing more managed information to enhance the existing knowledge base. Modern information technology plays a key role in this transitional development by building a knowledge infrastructure that can be developed and accessed not only internally but also globally.

Time Investment Required

The time spent creating or sharing knowledge is nearly impossible to justify in today's short-term oriented business environment. This point is extremely critical and not fully understood or accepted by management. With the excessive short-run orientation on the part of management, employees are forced into spending many hours on their jobs; hence, learning is almost an impossibility. Thus, learning is being ignored by the pressures of the moment. If more corporations are evaluated on a quarterly basis, it certainly becomes difficult to justify such a long-range soft investment return such as corporate learning. Unless top management explicitly frees up employees' time for the purpose of learning, there will be no progress in the area of corporate learning. If encouraging learning does not become part of the corporate culture, there will be very little (if any) knowledge creation and knowledge absorption at the individual level. Unless the rewards of taking time to create and add new knowledge to the organization's information base are greater than their inconvenience, there will be little progress.

Team Orientation

If an organization embraces teamwork, the idea of developing a learning organization becomes an easier transition. The idea of teamwork, by definition, is to share knowledge and to work together toward a common goal. The key to team success is interaction. It has been stated that interactive communities contribute to the amplification and development of new knowledge. The team also needs to share knowledge and experiences with the organization. Future organizations are most likely to be composed of task-oriented teams using the majority of resources within the organization. If the company does not have a team orientation, it will be rather difficult if not impossible to train every member of the organization individually to share knowledge and work within teams. Experts believe that the people who work best in a knowledge-sharing environment are team-oriented, and allowing them to become part of a team is necessary.

Usage of Knowledge Within the Organization

A learning organization will use accumulated knowledge for its decisions and their outcomes. The quality of the knowledge and how well it is used in business decisions are the key indicators that the organization is actively learning. If the knowledge is of high quality and used effectively, the overall performance of the firm in the marketplace will improve. This improvement can be measured by changes in the profit picture, market share, or sales volume. Internally, increased employee satisfaction may indicate the same positive knowledge-use pattern. Decisions need to be based on combined organizational knowledge. This way, knowledge delivers greater value to clients faster, and provides correct solutions to all involved. The feedback and results of corporate decisions provide additional knowledge that should go into the knowledge repositories of the firm to facilitate future decisions.

DEMOCRATIZATION OF INFORMATION

The vision of the top management about the company's future, its markets, its alternative courses of action, and, above all, its reasoning based on the information generated cannot be shared with just a privileged few. The information must be shared by all so that everyone will feel an important part of the organization and be motivated to accomplish the vision and the goals. It is not the compelling vision of the top management, but understanding the brutal facts of the market and proposed solutions by all that will make a difference.[7]

CRITICAL COUNTERCHAOS CHECKLIST

1. Do we have a learning organization?
2. Are we suffering from a data overload and an information underload?
3. Do we know how to accumulate and manage knowledge?
4. Do we democratize information by sharing it with our team members?
5. Is the critical information where it is supposed to be during the decision process?

SUMMARY

This chapter deals with a very critical factor in counteracting chaos in the marketplace. First it is posited that the firm must have a strategic information system (SIS), which has six key steps: direct, collect, process, generate, disseminate, and use. But, above all, the firm must be a learning organization that proactively generates information and uses it effectively. Ten key aspects of a learning organization are discussed in the remainder of the chapter. These 10 features of a learning organization are: organizational leadership, internal communication, type of resources utilized, amount of quality research, mobility of the corporate culture, degree of interaction among corporate offices, technical architecture, time investment required, team orientation, and use of knowledge within the organization. It is maintained here that if these 10 features or factors are intact, then the company will have the capability to cope with the unexpected market shocks by proper *improvisation.*

Chapter 7

The Art and Science of Improvisation

Our discussion thus far revolves around being futuristic, being sensitive to unexpected market conditions, detecting danger quickly, and responding to danger signs in a nonconventional manner. Everincreasing market adversities and variations in these adversities necessitate managements that are trying to develop counterchaos skills to deal with the unexpected and, more critically, with the unknown. Therein lies the importance of improvisation. The concept is derived from a Latin word "*improvisus,*" which means, "not seen ahead of time." It combines two key aspects of decision-making, planning, and implementation. But the critical aspect of improvisation is that planning and implementation are performed simultaneously for something that was not seen ahead of time. Thus, improvisation can be seen as a link between planning the predictable and responding to the unpredictable at the same time. Here we can look at the market as a continual state of flux, and we can look at improvisation as a continual state of development and redevelopment.[1] Organizational learning that is discussed in Chapter 6 must facilitate improvisation by providing information both in terms of planning and implementation.

IMPROVISATION PLANNING

It is necessary to build a general framework for the antecedents and consequences of improvisation in organizational counterchaos strategies. Antecedents of improvisation such as memory, different types of environmental turbulence, and the speed of information flow will provide also a series of consequences of improvisation. While a deliberate plan of

Figure 7.1.
The Three Phases of Improvisation Planning.

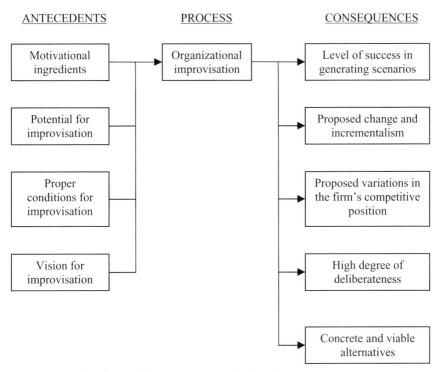

Source: Adapted and revised from Vieira daCunha (1999).

improvisation needs to be developed very quickly, what Murphy and Murphy (2003) posit is also quite appropriate. They propose "making haste slowly," meaning that no matter how much in a hurry the corporation is in, without carefully thinking and planning the antecedents and consequences of the improvisation activity, nothing can happen. Here not only a very speedy improvisation plan must be prepared, but a variety of scenarios may be aimed at so that the ones that will bring success are hit quickly. Since, at the organizational level, improvisation means continuous exploration and experimentation, a general framework for improvisation planning must be established and must be utilized effectively. Improvisation planning as presented here has three phases: antecedents, process, and consequences (Figure 7.1).

Antecedents

In order for the firm to be involved in effective improvisation, which is perhaps the most powerful tool in coping with chaos, critical antecedents for the improvisation process must be established. Four groups of antecedents must be present for a healthy organizational improvisation culture to be present: motivational ingredients, potential for improvisation, proper conditions for improvisation, and vision for improvisation.

Motivational ingredients of improvisation may be considered event-specific. An event such as a major market disturbance or a chaotic development occurs. If there has been a corporate culture of improvisation, event readiness is the first factor. Of course, all events do not have an equal impact on the corporation; therefore, the degree of importance of the event to our company would determine the intensity of the improvisation that is likely to take place. An event can be very difficult or rather easy to cope with. If the important event is also difficult, then a sense of urgency sets in. All four—readiness, importance, difficulty, and urgency—become a very powerful motivation for improvisation.

The potential for improvisation is determined by the organization's structure. If structurally the organization is composed of more than one group and if these groups have major differences in thinking and acting, improvisation may become easier. Similarly, if the level of real-time information is very high, the firm's potential for improvisation is enhanced. Although every event is different, the corporation could have a very pervasive memory of what procedures took place in the last event-related improvisation. Finally, the improvisational potential is strongly enhanced with the presence of what may be called an action culture.

Finally, in addition to the first three groups' antecedents, a vision for improvisation must be present. A sense of meaningful risk-taking and a sense of thinking out of the box are necessary ingredients to facilitate the improvisation activity.

Process

Since improvisation is seen as an unplanned but rather purposeful and deliberate response to a particular turbulence in a dynamic environment, it may be considered a major option. The process of improvisation, therefore, is critically dependent on the immediacy of planning that initiates the activity availability and proper utilization of the corporate resources to handle the task that the planning specified. It must clearly display an authoritative intent of certain outcome within a certain cost parameter.

Consequences

The consequences of the improvisation planning activity must be such that it can generate multiple scenarios. Each one of these proposed scenarios would imply different degrees of *major* changes in the corporation's marketing activity and market positioning. Conversely the scenarios may imply a variety of incremental changes in the company's marketing undertakings. The proposed major or incremental changes in the marketing activity based on the improvisation process would indicate variations in the firm's competitive position. Assessing such expected variations would enable management to choose among scenarios. The degree of deliberateness of the proposed scenarios needs to be considered so that the proactive novelty that is conceptualized by the improvisation process can be assertively implemented. Finally, the alternative or scenarios generated by the improvisation process must clearly show high degrees of concreteness and viability. Figure 7.1 presents the characteristics of the three stages of improvisation, that is, antecedents, process, and consequences. Perhaps the time element is most critical in the improvisation process.

SPEED TO MARKET: A MOST POWERFUL TOOL

Both in planning and implementation of improvised options, time needs to be put into the forefront. In at least three key sequential events in the total process, time emerges as a very critical factor. First, early detection of the market disturbance that causes the initiation of the improvisation process is required. If the market disturbance is not detected early enough, counteracting it successfully becomes less likely. Second, the whole planning process of improvisation must be accomplished as quickly as possible within the constraints of, as Murphy and Murphy[2] would coin, "making haste somewhat slowly." In other words, if the improvised scenario that reaches the market is not quite ready to be implemented and not carefully thought out, the benefits of speed will be totally wasted by the inadequacy of actions. Thus, rushing into action is good but not prematurely. And third, the outcome of the improvisation process must reach the market as quickly as possible.

Studies have shown that team improvisation facilitates speed-to-market without which the firm may have extreme difficulty coping with chaotic market conditions. It must be reiterated that behind speed-to-market, there is motivation to improvise and potential to improvise. Speed-to-market is considered to be one of the ultimate competitive weapons.[3]

THE NEW PARADIGM OF INNOVATION

Both motivation to improvise and the potential to improvise will be challenged to innovate. As mentioned earlier, customer preferences are changing rapidly, technological developments are increasing exponentially, and information from markets is becoming readily available. These key factors are necessary to think out of the box, that is, improvise and, clearly, innovate accordingly. The connection, if any, between improvisation and innovation must be carefully articulated.

It is certainly possible to be innovative without improvisation. Companies such as Motorola and 3M are known by their innovativeness and their ability to generate new products.

However, the new products generated are not necessary to take advantage or at least counteract market turbulence. It is maintained here that, assuming the improvisation process is effective, innovation stimulated with improvisation is likely to be more effective as a response to chaotic market events. Thus, it is posited that improvisation-stimulated innovation is more innovating for the future than improving on the past. If improvisation is totally nonexistent, the probabilities are greater for the innovation efforts going in the direction of improving on the past. In the final analysis, if the firm does not have any innovativeness, the increasing adversities in the marketplace are likely to destroy it.

CAN WE MAKE INNOVATION HAPPEN?

Organizations in dynamic markets need to innovate. Innovations not only in terms of new products and services but also in terms of different types of communication, different types of pricing, and even different types of distribution, must be considered, developed, and delivered. Understanding just what drives successful innovation, therefore, is critical. Creativity, in a sense, is a critical property of the thought process. It may be acquired and improved through practice and knowledge that facilitate innovation which, in turn, enhances the individual's or the organization's capability of developing something new, different, or powerful that would enhance the market position of the firm. Figure 7.2 illustrates how innovation fits into the performance of the company. According to the diagram, innovativeness is advanced by improvisation, previously discussed, and also by vision. Vision is a powerful contributor to the innovativeness of the firm. The term vision is derived from a Latin word, "*vide*," to see. It combines knowledge with foresight. It implies some desired future state such as "our firm has enough survival experience to react promptly to an unexpected market aberration." The vision can be much more specific and clear than the above statement. Such specificity and clarity would provide the firm's innovativeness an important and very necessary direction.[4]

Figure 7.2.
Innovativeness and Performance.

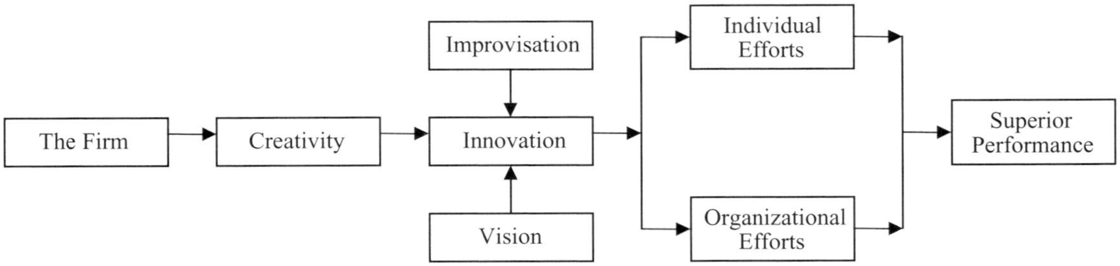

| The Firm | → | Creativity | → | Innovation | → | Individual Efforts | → | Superior Performance |

Improvisation → Innovation ← Vision

Individual Efforts → Superior Performance
Organizational Efforts → Superior Performance

The combined characteristics and related activities of creativity, improvisation, and vision are practiced by individuals in the organization individually as well as the corporation itself. It must be emphasized that the organizations that encourage such practices individually as well as part of a futuristic corporate culture simultaneously synergize the total innovativeness of the firm that leads to superior performance in the marketplace.

SPEED TO MARKET, ONCE AGAIN

The discussion of this new paradigm of innovation without a doubt pays off generously as the whole activity accelerates the speed to market. But it must be reiterated that in the new paradigm of innovation, improvisation plays a very different and critical role. Not only does it improve the firm's agility to respond to chaotic market pressures, but it also shortens the response time of the firm to the market disruption. Improvisation, above all, can accelerate the firm's speed to market with its most recent innovations.

Since improvisation, if developed and utilized properly, is a powerful tool to cope with the unexpected and prepares the firm to react quickly to chaotic market changes and can facilitate this reaction in a proactive manner, it is rather indispensable.

MOVING FROM "PLANNING FOR THE PREDICTABLE" TO "RESPONDING TO THE UNPREDICTABLE"

One can argue that during the second half of the 20th century, corporations have spent more time and energy for future planning. Much of the forecasting techniques relied on what has transpired in the recent past. We have developed powerful statistical techniques to predict the future based on the past. In essence, we functioned on the premise that history does and indeed will repeat itself. Thus much effort has been spent on different versions of time series analyses and exponential techniques used to analyze time series. Such preoccupation with the past gave rise to "winning formulas" that are outdated almost at the point of their inception. Certainly, it is critical to understand how we got here. But future is not necessarily a function of the past or present. Surely our past and present performance has some impact in forming some aspects of the future, but emphasizing the future as an entity within itself, which it is, and planning for it, indeed as stated earlier, innovating the future of the firm requires different ways of thinking.

Indeed present and future are connected, but trying to accommodate the future as it becomes a fully bloomed reality is too late. Instead, the futuristic orientation calls for detecting early indicators. There are direct and indirect early indicators, detection of which can help our company to innovate its own future.

In Chapter 4, a discussion of early indicators or symptoms is presented. Here an attempt is made to distinguish between direct and indirect early indicators. There can be innumerable examples of both direct and indirect early indicators. The critical point is to be able to identify and prioritize them. All indicators, after all, are not equally important and, hence, it will take much understanding of the market and much sensitivity about the market forces that are influencing our business. Based on the detected and prioritized indicators, continuous exploration and continuous experimentation are pursued in conjunction with improvisation. If, for instance, our company is engaged in production of many food lines and if more fattening lines are not selling well, this is a direct early indicator. Simultaneously, if healthy food lines and food supplements are starting to sell heavily, for our company this would be indirect early indicators.

Continuous exploration into total improvisation activity requires developing multiple product line concepts along with continuous experimentation, exploring how these product line concepts may be marketed.

IMPROVISATION AS A STRATEGY

From our discussion so far, it is clear that improvisation can easily be a major game plan for companies functioning at the cutting edge of very dynamic markets. Companies must develop a knowledge base on procedural and declarative memories. While the procedural memory deals with how the previous improvisation processes progressed and developed, the declarative memory deals with the implementation of these improvisation processes. Learning how improvisations become more successful is in itself an important activity. The knowledge based on managing and implementing improvisation successfully is not widespread in marketing and management literature; however, this particular strategic option will be more and more valuable as markets become more and more chaotic.

IMPROVISATION VERSUS CONVENTIONAL WISDOM

It is maintained here that improvisations are futuristic, proactive, and critical in surviving chaotic times. While conventional wisdom

(Chapter 3) is attempting to improve the present performance, improvisation truly facilitates innovating for the future. Although it is possible to innovate without improvisation, it is rather questionable if such an activity can clearly become futuristic and proactive. Innovations based on improvisation almost by definition are futuristic and proactive.[5]

The Secret of 37 Signals LLC

The 37 Signals LLC is a small Chicago company with an ironclad rule of: never take more than 3 1/2 months to generate a new product. The company maintains that this is the model to run a company well. Instead of planning, the creative workers of the firm just start creating and trying things out. They make sure that the products can do a few things well. The company's principle to develop really good software is to make the simplest thing you can as fast as possible so that you can get reaction so that it can be improved. The company is beyond focus groups and standard market research. Screening and evaluating new ideas is going in the direction of being in touch with online networks and interacting with experts worldwide. In some ways the company can be labeled as a permanent improviser.[6]

CRITICAL COUNTERCHAOS CHECKLIST

1. Do we realize that our market is in a continual state of flux?
2. Do we realize that in a continual state of flux improvisation means continual development?
3. Do we have capabilities and plans for improvisation?
4. Would improvisation bring about new products or services that can be taken to the market speedily?
5. How can we develop an improvisational strategy?

SUMMARY

This chapter deals with a very critical and neglected activity called improvisation. It combines two key aspects of decision-making: planning and implementation. In improvisation, these two key aspects of decision-making are performed simultaneously. The corporate entity must develop the three phases of improvisation properly. The improvisation process leads to proactive and futuristic innovation that conventional wisdom cannot. Thus, corporations moving from planning the predictable to responding quickly and effectively to the unexpected market adversities must develop an experiential base to improvise so that the results satisfy the speed-to-market requirements.

Chapter 8

Products and Services in Generating Consumer Value

The true futuristic characteristics of a company are seen in its products or services. As market adversities accelerate, some companies' products or services cease generating consumer value. This is when the company has to act even if it does not have detailed plans of action. Since such situations occur suddenly and unexpectedly, the company must have a product-service strategy that could overcome such devastating occurrences and convert the situation into a winning proposition swiftly. As chaotic conditions set in, consumers alter their attitudes toward buying and consuming products. In this process, they could easily forget our products and go for new, better, or cheaper similarities.

Most companies regularly develop new products. While many of these products are "incremental" developments within the firm's merchandise mix, some of them are rather radical developments that may also be coined as "breakthroughs." In order to understand the difference between these two almost diametrically opposing approaches, we must examine the market opportunities.

PRODUCT INNOVATION AND MARKET OPPORTUNITIES

Any kind of product innovation is costly and hence is risky, but in our market system, there is almost a parallel between risk and profitability. The greater the risk, the greater is the profitability. Table 8.1 illustrates four separate scenarios that a firm is likely to encounter.[1]

Table 8.1
Product-Market Opportunities

Scenario	Product Development Function	Time Frame	Risk Factor	Description of the Orientation
Scenario 1: (M+P+) Market is ready, recognizable, and there are numerous products in existence to satisfy this need.	Imitative designs either complementary or substituting for existing products.	Very short-run	Low-risk activity. Short-run, positive ROIs.*	Minimal incremental product development.
Scenario 2: (M+P−) Although there are clear-cut needs, there are no readily available products.	Modifying design either by expanding product line or deviating from it along with some innovation.	Short-run	Intermediate risk activity. Short-run to intermediate run, good ROIs.	Incremental product development
Scenario 3: (M−P+) Through existing research and development and technology new products are being developed. However, there is no obvious market for these products.	Innovative designs either taking existing innovations and developing new products or simultaneously creating new products as by-products of others developed.	Intermediate- to long-run	High-risk activity. Possibly numerous high ROIs, but only a few will be very high.	Varies between incremental and radical
Scenario 4: (M−P−) Ongoing basic research may one day lead to development of new markets.	Basic research emphasis leading to major breakthroughs and inventions.	Very long-run	Very high-risk activity. Great ROIs if product developed.	Radical product development counterchaos capability

* ROI = Return on Investment.
Source: Adapted and revised from Samli (1993).

Scenario One

Business opportunities often revolve around a market for an existing product. This was the case when Burger King entered the market that was dominated by McDonald's, when Pepsi-Cola challenged Coca-Cola, Dannon started competing with Yoplait, or a million other examples. The products are very similar here, and entry into the market is through imitation or complementation of the existing products, substituting a new product that is new and better than the existing ones such as substituting TVs with, say, high-density television. The orientation in this case is short run. The new product is likely to be a fast-learning type. Microwaveable popcorn, for instance, can be considered fast-learning. Similarly, however, because people are, in general, familiar with McDonald's, they may accept or reject Burger King quickly. There is reasonably low risk involved in this minimal incremental product development activity. Along with low risk, there is also limited return on investment. However, many companies are engaged in this type of product innovation activity. Product innovation is the single most important factor in developing competitive advantage. It is giving the firm something unique that its competitors do not have.[2] In this stage of analysis, the activity may be a simple extension, easily introduced, and reasonably profitable.

Scenario Two

This is a typical short-run challenge in the most familiar sense of the marketing concept. It involves a potential market whose characteristics are deduced by the information collected from potential buyers. Consumer research indicates clearly that there are unsatisfied needs, and such needs represent markets for new products. Here the new product development process takes place, which involves idea generation, screening, concept specification, prototype development, market testing, and finally commercialization. In such situations, product design, typically, is deviation from existing products, such as generating an apparel line for oversize people. Thus, the degree of innovation is rather minimal. Since the market is already present and the product is not too difficult to adjust to market needs, the level of risk is not very high. It may be considered slightly higher than scenario one, above. If successful, this approach to incremental product development would yield relatively high return on investment in the short run. Development and marketing of, say, one-a-day vitamins for women or for those who are over the age of 50, is a typical example of this scenario.

Scenario Three

Perhaps in recent years we have seen more examples of this scenario. This is because there have been many notable advances in technology and, as such, there have been and are many *technology-driven* products. The development of the Internet, for instance, has given rise to many software products.

Either based on existing innovative designs as starting points and developing new products or simultaneously creating new products as by-products of other emerging new products, this scenario is rather noticeably active. Although many products developed in this manner may not be all that successful, many very successful products also emerged. The chip in the electronic industry facilitated many new versions of existing products as well as many new products, such as high density TV, cell phones, digital cameras, and so on. These products did require intermediate to long-run development, and are high-risk activity. Many products in this category vary between being incremental or radical developments. The more radical they are, the higher risk they represent.

Scenario Four

Some U.S. firms spend large sums of money on basic research, hoping to generate breakthroughs. Basic research does not yield specific commercial results all the time, but it can. Today, from stem cell research to fuel cell research, a tremendous variety of basic research is being conducted. It is difficult to predict what kinds of products may emerge from such activity, but the costs are definitely very high, and results may take much longer to materialize. The outcome typically is a series of radical product developments. Not only are the probabilities of generating breakthroughs very low, but originally the results of basic research becoming a number of viable products is a high-risk activity all by itself. But, companies that are capable of developing radical products can make much money. Above all, they have the first mover advantage that provides a powerful market superiority position.

Thus, on a spectrum, product development moves from evolutionary to revolutionary as indicated by the above four scenarios. However, the product development process can be separated into two separate pathways. Figure 8.1 illustrates these two critical pathways. Scenarios one, two, and partially three, deal with evolutionary product innovation. They indicate incremental developments, while scenario three, partially, and scenario

Figure 8.1.
Product Development Pathway.

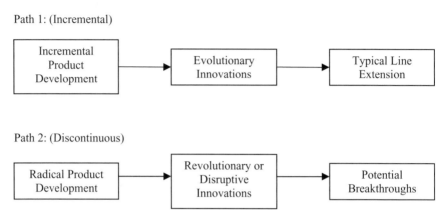

Path 1: (Incremental)

Path 2: (Discontinuous)

four deal with revolutionary product innovation. It represents the thinking of radical product developments leading to breakthroughs.

Path 1 in Figure 8.1 deals with the extension of conventional wisdom. Incremental product development leading to product line extension is the typical product development activity in our market system. It is critical to realize that not only are such developments not very profitable, but they also could not protect the firm against sudden and spectacular market developments.

DISCONTINUOUS PRODUCT DEVELOPMENT

As was discussed earlier in Chapter 4, the chaos theory posits that relationships in complex systems such as markets are nonlinear. In other words, the relationships are disruptive and shocking. Traditionally, it has been stated that firms periodically must also be engaged in disruptive and revolutionary innovation for long-term survival.[3] However, one must question two key implications of such a statement. First, an occasional or casual disruptive-revolutionary innovation program may not coincide with the disruptive events of the market system, which need to be addressed immediately. It would be rather a miracle to manage the coinciding feature of the firm's disruptive innovation program with the developments in the market if the firm is not agile and does not think out of the box.

Second, being periodically engaged in disruptive innovation for long-term survival is a questionable stance. In chaotic times, the firm must cope with chaotic shock waves in the short run. Once again, if the market displays a shockingly different desire in the short run, the firms must be able to react effectively and swiftly. Thus, the "traditional position" can be criticized seriously.

As opposed to what is coined as the traditional thinking above, the opposite needs to be considered. First, counteracting disruptive events in the market should be achieved not by *occasional* disruptive innovation but a *continuous* effort to generate disruptive innovations, and/or by generating new and unusual luxury products, in other words, a discipline of continuous effort leading to radical product development. Such effort enables a firm to react forcefully to the disruptive or chaotic market developments because it is ready for them. Second, this continuous effort to generate disruptive innovations is not for survival in the long run but survival and success in the *short run*. In other words, lasik surgery came about as a reaction to disposable contact lenses, or free greeting cards downloadable over the Internet as a reaction to printed greeting cards. Thus, discontinuous or disruptive innovation activity goes on or *at least* must go on. When "all of a sudden a competitor comes along and changes the market landscape like a lightning bolt,"[4] if we don't have a program of discontinuing or disruptive innovation, we cannot deal with this current disaster. Left alone, another one is just around the corner.

EVALUATING PRODUCT IDEAS

Although consumers are the final judges in the marketplace as to which products go and which products stay, they are not the final word in terms of their needs. In fact, purely consumer-evaluated new product concepts may be handicapped in the sense that they may be further away from the consumers' realm of reality; hence, they have less chance to become a reality.[5] Here there is always a conflict between present and future. Typically, due to traditional evaluation processes and because of conventional wisdom, disruptive or more futuristic products have less chance to become a reality. In short, traditional companies that are run by conventional wisdom opt more for the present than the future. Whether we opt for present or for future, it is critical to have an effective process in place.

NEW PRODUCT IDEA EVALUATION PROCESS

The conflict between present and future must be taken very seriously. Companies that are entering the market from the upper end need to be more futuristic as opposed to those entering the market from the lower end. It is obvious that Bloomingdales has to make more of an impact in regard to new designs and styles than does Wal-Mart. Similarly, Hewlett-Packard or IBM, since they enter the market from the upper end, have to have more tendency to develop and introduce disruptive products than Dell, which happens to enter the market from the lower end. It may be articulated that as far as the above description of the high-tech market positioning is concerned, Dell is likely to be more vulnerable to market-induced chaos. Under the dictates of such an orientation, Dell is putting all of its efforts (or almost all of its efforts) into making the product and process cheaper and more efficient so that it can establish a cost-price leadership. Obviously, Dell is putting much more emphasis on incremental product development by using *sustaining* as opposed to *disruptive* technologies. In other words, unlike HP and IBM, Dell has more at stake in the sustaining technologies. This orientation can be described as an extension of conventional wisdom and would be very profitable under nonchaotic market conditions. Indeed, even under the chaotic pressures of an economic downturn, emphasizing sustaining technologies and emphasizing the present with incremental developments, Dell's orientation can be very profitable. Only a major question remains unanswered: Could Dell do as well as, say, IBM or HP if there were major disruptive technologies and commensurate products were causing chaos? If Dell is functioning at the levels of scenarios one and two in Table 8.1, it is more vulnerable to market adversities than scenarios three and four. This may be one outcome of dealing with the present as opposed to dealing with the future. It is obvious that a company must deal both with the present as well as the future. Dealing with the present and the future both in the same or different proportions becomes an extremely critical activity. The company must have a product or a product line that the market desires and accepts so that it can survive at the present time. However, if it is not futuristic, it may only be short-lived. Polaroid had a very revolutionary product that was widely accepted by the market. However, by the time the company reached the end of its patent right, it did not have any futuristic new products. All of its competitors had better products, and the rest is history. The company does not exist anymore. Thus, we must manage the present first but, as has been stated previously, the future is not a simple extension of the present and we, therefore, must innovate for the future.

Present management of innovation deals with numerous products that were evaluated as ideas some time ago and now are actual products. In managing innovation both in the present and the future, it must be realized that it takes some time and a number of functions before a product moves from the ideation stage to becoming a market reality. Needless to say, there is more time to develop futuristic products, but in the final analyses both types of innovations must benefit from a speedy behavior.

MANAGING PRESENT PRODUCT NEEDS

Perhaps, above all, it must be stated that even though, in the final analysis, consumers decide which products survive in the marketplace, purely consumer-evaluated new product concepts may be quite handicapped because if they are not within close proximity to the consumers' realm of reality, they are not likely to be approved by consumers. Thus, traditional evaluation processes may not give equal opportunity to more futuristic and far-out new product ideas. This is another reason why conventional wisdom is under suspicion.[6] But even in the short-run, such as in scenario two of Table 8.1, some products may go through a more major revision or modification to cater to consumer needs. Here the degree of uniqueness is critical and must be handled with care. Figure 8.2 presents a modified procedure of what is typically found in textbooks.

The first modification of the exhibit is in the idea-generation stage. New ideas can come from within the corporation or from government, universities, or jointly sponsored research efforts among others. Here, most importantly, the idea generation is assumed to follow some serious basic research and improvisation as discussed in Chapter 7, so that truly innovative product concepts can emerge.

Internal feasibility assessment is the second step. Here many ideas are eliminated because the company administrators may feel that they are not feasible or, at least, they are not in the company's *core competency* area. Most of the time decisions here are made in favor of line extensions or brand extensions that call for smaller basic investment or are more suitable for existing facilities or characteristics of the firm. In other words, they represent conventional wisdom expanding the present rather than innovating for the future. It is maintained here that future-oriented ideas must also get proper attention.

Both concept testing and specification of the features of the proposed new product idea need to be achieved by future focus groups carefully composed of future-oriented and sophisticated people who can distinguish latent needs from current and identified needs. Such focus groups, unlike the current practice, need to be composed of scientists, corporate executives, and specially selected customers, such as consumer advocates and business professors.

In the market-testing stage, it is also maintained here that we use unusual consumers. These consumers must be *innovators* and early adopters, since

Figure 8.2.
The Product Idea Evaluation Process.

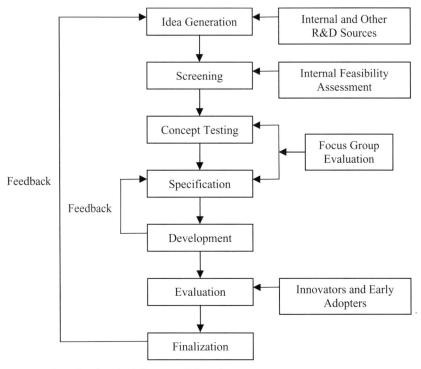

Source: Adapted and revised from Samli (1993).

typical ordinary consumers have difficulty relating to products that are significantly different than their predecessors. Consumer innovators have been described in numerous studies. They are better educated than average, highly exposed to mass media, socially active, opinion leaders, cosmopolitan, and venturesome.[7] Along with being experts and heavy users of related products, they can effectively evaluate technology-pushed product ideas as well. Although there are practical difficulties in finding and grouping these consumers into focus groups, this certainly becomes an important undertaking.

The future-focused group concept must be embraced by the company and must be utilized carefully, since these groups are most likely to perform better than other groups in assessing the success possibilities of new products. Although a number of techniques have been developed or suggested to construct such innovator panels as future-focused groups, each company still needs to develop the details of such activities individually. When we expect a realistic assessment of the product in question, there should not only be a very accurate visual description, but also a detailed outline of the product's potential use.[8]

Finally, in addition to using specially constituted consumer groups for concept testing as well as market testing, certain nonconventional techniques need to be used in dealing with these groups. One such technique is *Hedonic Analysis.* This analysis probes into multisensory fantasy and emotive aspects related to the ownership and use of the proposed new product. This technique is particularly useful when testing products that are innovative or futuristic. Similarly, research indicates that *market transaction data* can be used to estimate the demand for product characteristics. Indicating the direction and trends in consumer consumption patterns, such information would affirm acceptable features of the proposed new product. Finally, the *laddering technique* could connect the concrete attributes of the proposed products to much broader and intangible socioeconomic and psychological consumer values. These are only three of possibly many other approaches in dealing with future-focused groups regarding new and innovative product ideas.

It must be reiterated that there is a major time gap between the product ideation and actual physical introduction of the product to the market. Hence, even though we might be dealing with present product portfolio, since there is a time lapse in the development of the proposed product development activities, it is necessary to be reasonably futuristic even in the short run. But the situation becomes more critical if we are managing not a present, but a futuristic portfolio.

MANAGING FUTURISTIC PORTFOLIOS

Regardless of the nature, size, or shape of the company, all firms must have some semblance of a futuristic product portfolio. This is not only appropriate for managing the future but also having some degree of readiness against chaotic influences or changes in the marketplace. Figure 8.3 presents a model of constructing a future product portfolio. Such a portfolio has four distinct phases as discussed below.

PHASE ONE

This phase is particularly critical since only good ideas lead to development of good products. The model presents five key sources of possible product ideas.

Figure 8.3.
The Process of Developing A Futuristic Product Portfolio.

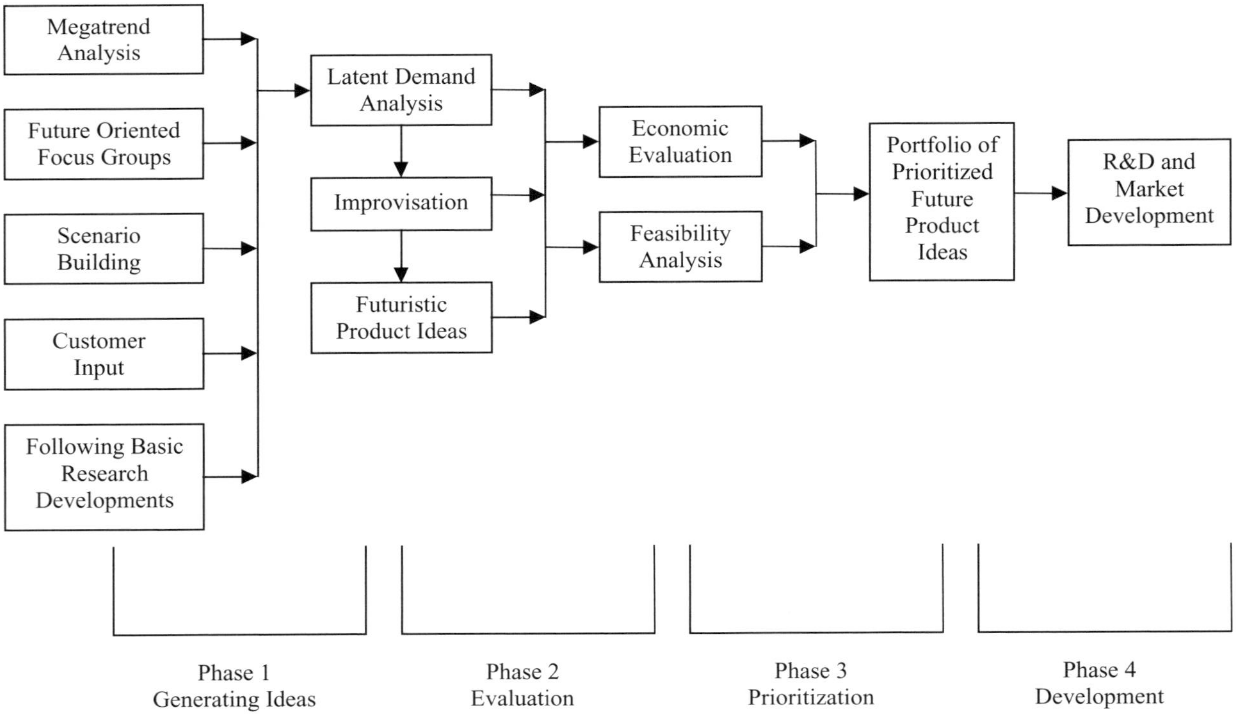

Megatrend Analysis

There are always megatrends in the making. If detected carefully, they can be implemented into new product development efforts. The emerging megatrend of health consciousness has encouraged the development of multitudinous products and services, from health food supplements, to exercise equipment, to diet control programs. Understanding megatrends necessarily leads to conceptualization of futuristic products. Because of its importance, this topic is discussed in greater detail later on in this chapter.

Future-Focused Groups

This concept has been explored earlier in this chapter. Suffice it to say here that future-focused groups composed of *innovators* and *early adopters* can produce very valuable sets of ideas in generating product concepts to materialize some time in the future.

Scenario Building

This is a technique that has been used in long-range forecasting. An attempt is made here to foresee future changes in an industry. By first monitoring the environment, existing and emerging external changes are identified. The resultant strategic and significant industry-related issues are pinpointed. These issues are then analyzed to create scenarios of what the business climate will be in the industry, three, five, or more years ahead. Usually, multiple scenarios are developed and are all based on the assumptions made about the speed, timing, and impact of the identified changes.

Once a set of scenarios is created, the one that the management thinks is likely to occur is selected. From this scenario, deductions are made regarding the possible changes in current markets and new market opportunities that may emerge. From these possible changes, along with emerging new markets, futuristic product ideas are expected to emerge.

There are at least two differences between the megatrends and scenario-building methodologies. First, scenarios are relatively more focused on changes in an industry. Environmental monitoring searches for changes in trends relevant to an industry, while megatrend research focuses on the implications of a broad trend in society. Second, scenarios are developed by company planners, while megatrends are often identified by people outside the company. Thus, these two techniques differ significantly, but they can easily be used in a complementary manner.

Customer Input

Solicited as well as unsolicited input from customers could be very valuable, not only in improving existing products and services, but also in generating new products and services. All firms must be in a position to receive and evaluate such input. After all, current customers are the most hands-on people regarding the firm's products. They could easily generate some important futuristic product ideas.

Basic Research Developments

Many nonprofit organizations such as the National Science Foundation (NSF) or National Institutes of Health (NIH), along with numerous universities, are engaged in basic research. Results of such research, for instance, the human genome project, or nanotechnologies, may have tremendous implications for new product possibilities. A direct connection to basic research activities throughout the country or the world can definitely enhance the possibilities of expanding the futuristic product portfolio for the firm.

The second part of phase one in futuristic product portfolio development is the ideation stage. The possible ideas generated from the first group of key sources in Figure 8.3 must become a list of new product ideas. Developing such a list has at least three specific steps: latent demand analysis, improvisation, and futuristic product idea generation.

Almost all of the five key information sources must be connected to latent demand. If, for instance, the megatrend indicates more health consciousness, a company that is dealing with food processing can have multiple futuristic product ideas. Here improvisation and thinking out of the box becomes very important in terms of, say, food supplements, in what form, and how they will be delivered.

Finally the first phase of generating a futuristic portfolio is completed as a number of futuristic product ideas are developed. Here each idea will have to have some very specific descriptions about its concrete attributes and how they may connect to personal values in the minds of consumers, as laddering would necessitate.

PHASE TWO

Phase two of the futuristic portfolio development is related to the evaluation of the futuristic product ideas that will be subsequently included in the portfolio. The ideas generated in phase one will be evaluated from an economic perspective as well as the feasibility of such an idea. Economic evaluation is rather straightforward. Approximating the current value of expected future revenues of the proposed product and comparing it with expected total costs is the general approach. Feasibility analysis, on the other hand, delves into approximating if the proposed product fits into the core competency area of the firm. If not, what would it take to develop competency to handle the new product. Needless to say, this whole evaluation process will be repeated for all the proposed futuristic product ideas.

PHASE THREE

A number of futuristic product ideas, after the evaluation process, will become the firm's futuristic product portfolio. However, the entrants into the futuristic portfolio do not have the same level of importance. They may need to be evaluated as stars, question marks, and perhaps cash cows. Obviously there is no reason to include dogs in such a portfolio. The firm will have to decide where to put its resources to make this futuristic portfolio a reality. Just how do we evaluate entrants into this futuristic product portfolio? This is a very difficult question. The perceptions of latent demands, along with successes by the research and development group in addition to the results of improvisation, can give a good indication.

PHASE FOUR

As the prioritization activity is completed and the futuristic portfolio is constructed, the most promising stars may be put into the firm's R&D activity. As these products are developed, the market development of the activity would receive special attention. Alerting, informing, and cultivating the carefully identified target markets are necessary activities for smooth introduction of the futuristic products as their time comes.

MORE ON MEGATRENDS

Naisbitt[9] popularized the concept of megatrends. Society is dynamic and always moving in the direction of major developments that are pretty much accepted by large groups or the masses. He presented 10 such trends that impacted our lives. Table 8.2 is based on these 10 megatrends and their

Table 8.2
From Megatrends to Futuristic Opportunities

Megatrend	Implication	Potential Futuristic Idea	Related Examples
1. From an industrial to an information society.	• Fast transfer of information to control manufacturing processes	• Robotics using expert systems in production sequences	• Using CAD and CAM in textile industry
2. From high-tech to high-touch	• The humanizing of high-tech and making it more acceptable in households	• Use of information in the home—supplemental people components to all high-tech developments	• Voice-activated computers • Home security systems that repel intruders
3. From self-sufficiency to global interdependence	• Identifying needs of global markets	• Developing products with global appeal • Global distribution of products	• An AIDs vaccine • A cure for cancer • Cheap sources of energy
4. Increasing long-term orientation by some CEOs	• Awareness of need for a futuristic orientation	• Finding technological breakthroughs for new lines of business	• Biogenetics • G-nome • The Internet • Nanotechnologies
5. From top-down to bottom-up management processes in companies	• Ability to communicate with larger groups of people and moving information quickly	• Visual interactive conference systems • Cell phones • Hand-held computers	• Visual telephone systems • E-mail • The Internet • Fast copiers

6. Deemphasizing help from outside, emphasizing self-reliance	• Greater need for personal self-sufficiency	• Home self-training programs in medical needs and do-it-yourself projects • Interactive gardening, home repair, and computer-use kits	• Home-exercise tapes • Computer-use programs
7. Greater power for people in government, business, and marketplace	• Extended ability to participate in the political process	• Extensive two-way communication systems in towns and communities	• Advances in information technology • E-tailing
8. From hierarchies to networks	• Greater ability to generate and maintain alliances	• Effective communications systems between groups • Accelerate voice-activated Internet	• Better systems of conferencing • Advances in IT
9. Population shifts	• Major lifestyle changes • Economic programs for improvement	• DVDs • Home entertainment centers • Home robotics	• Computerized homes • Energy efficiency • Computerized distance-control of home operations • Modifiable sections in home architecture • Virtual reality before purchase
10. Increase demand for variety by consumers	• Ability to create mass customization • Generating more variety	• More efficient production systems dealing with small volumes • Being in closer touch with consumers	• Modular music and information systems.

Source: Adapted and expanded from Naisbitt (1982).

impact on our lives. It is critical for a proactive and futuristic company not only to determine the implications of these megatrends on their business, but also to detect other megatrends that might influence their business.

From an Industrial to an Information Society

As we become more of an information society, generating and disseminating information becomes critical. Here many new unplanned and unexpected opportunities may be found. Computer-aided design (CAD) and computer-aided manufacturing (CAM) are examples as outcomes of this megatrend. It is expected that there will be many others.

From High-Tech to High-Touch

Overemphasis on high tech has made the need for more human activities noticeable. More emotional undertakings, more "human" components to high-tech developments, more spiritual activity and products, have become rather important. In this sense the puck in the future is likely to go in the direction of more and better services.

From Self-Sufficiency to Global Interdependence

Understanding the importance of global markets and catering to them have become important areas of activity. A variety of more globally oriented products will be needed in this area. There will be many more varieties of products and services offered in global markets that are not even in existence.

Increasing Long-Term Orientation by Some CEOs

Putting more emphasis on radical product developments, developing a futuristic product portfolio, and starting to think out of the box have become more common practices. Managing the future orientation is partially due to this megatrend. However, this megatrend is likely to go much further than we have experienced thus far.

From Top-Down to Bottom-Up

Democratization of information within the corporate entity, and more and better information technologies to communicate with larger numbers of people are the key outcomes. Receiving ideas from the people in the organization and getting them involved in the overall corporate strategic thinking are likely to be further emphasized.

Emphasizing Self-Reliance

This megatrend has caused an explosion in do-it-yourself types of activities. More self-help products, more learn-as-you-go types of activities are likely to be even more popular in the near future. Self-reliance on the part of the consumers would lead in the direction of many niche markets that would present new opportunities for those who are managing the future.

Greater Power for People

As almost part of the bottom-up concept discussed above, allowing consumers to vote for certain issues, products, and services is encouraged. Any technical developments that would encourage people's participation and information flow are likely to become important in the long run. Once again, this process will send the puck in most unexpected directions.

From Hierarchies to Networks

Establishing sustainable alliances is the critical outcome. Here, effective audiovisual systems, more information technologies, and more ability enhancement in interpersonal communications are critical. Numerous new products to facilitate these needs are likely to emerge.

Population Shifts

Population shifts, by definition, are generating changes in lifestyles and associated needs. From new designs in housing to urban mass transportation, these changes are likely to snowball. The concomitant impact on the need for new development is one of the most critical developers of new niche markets.

Increasing Demand for Variety

The more sophisticated consumer of the 21st century is requiring multiple alternatives in products and service choices. In all aspects of life, more informed and more sophisticated consumers would identify their preferences directly and indirectly. As discussed in Chapter 13, this megatrend

Figure 8.4.
A Service Portfolio.

	High Market Share Low	
High	**Star**	**Problem Child**
	Mostly educational. Regarding how to use the new product, how to treat it, how to maintain it. What additional uses may come out of it (Expansion).	Somewhat futuristic. Anticipatory. Easing the introduction and use of the new product. Very close and expensive customer interaction (growth and development).
Market Growth Rate	**Cash Cow**	**Dog**
	Standard maintenance. Routine and lower cost service. More based on relationship marketing. Continuation of established relationships and sensitivity to customer reactions (maintenance).	Simply bare minimums. Maintaining company reputation and image. Maintaining a modicum of relationship marketing. Promoting forthcoming products (decline).
Low		

leads in the direction of "new luxuries," which is perhaps one of the most critical new dimensions of the puck.

THE PRODUCT-SERVICE SYNERGISM

Every product has a service component. Whether we are managing the present product portfolio or the future one, we must plan the nature and extent of the service component that will accompany our products. This author believes that if product and service compositions are properly planned, they will create strong synergism to enhance the firm's market position.

In using a Boston Consulting Group (BCG) product portfolio, it is possible to identify the characteristics of services that are complementary to the product categories in such a portfolio. Figure 8.4 presents a product-related service portfolio. It must be noted that each service category is different and connected to the same product category identification. In other words, services must perform certain things for products that are identified as stars. If star products receive star service, this would create a synergistic situation. The exhibit, just as a standard BCG product portfolio, has four service categories. For instance, star services for star products are likely to be educational in respect to how the new product is used and for what additional function it may serve.

The cash cow services for cash cow products imply routine maintenance. The service contributes and enhances continuation of established relationships with customers.

The problem child services may be quite futuristic, trying to move a new product into star status. Strong customer interaction is a critical ingredient of this category of services.

Finally, services for the dog category have to be minimal. Here maintaining the company's reputation as the product is eliminated becomes an issue. Some relationship marketing is exercised here also.

It must also be reiterated that services are not only complementary additions to products, but in exclusively service organizations, they are also the focal point. Table 8.2 can be interpreted as services complementary to existing products as well as services as the company's only products.

SERVICE QUALITY COMPONENT

At least for a short while, as the product may be losing its market appeal, increased service quality may prolong that product's life cycle until another and better product is developed. Here the service component plays an important role rather than synergism to generate breathing space for the company to introduce a substitute for the product in question.

MASS CUSTOMIZATION-PRODUCT OR SERVICE

Again, one of the ways of prolonging the product's life cycle by improving service is *mass customization*. This concept implies the identification and fulfillment of the wants and needs of individual customers without sacrificing production efficiency and effectiveness, and without increasing costs to very high levels.[10] By personalizing the product characteristics, it becomes possible to keep customers happy, thereby prolonging the product's life cycle. Here, this author considers mass customization a very good working relationship between production and service.

The Case of Hand-Held Power Tools

A successful hand tool manufacturer was exploring its prospective growth market for the hand-held power tools that the company was developing. The company's development team produced and field-tested some prototypes with no success. The firm realized that its way of identifying customer needs was less than adequate. The company realized that it must predict customer needs even before customers are cognizant of them themselves. The company used a five-step research process to detect the forthcoming customer needs. These five steps included: gathering raw data from customers, interpreting this raw data in terms of customer needs, developing a priority ordering of these needs, establishing a relative importance of the prioritized needs, and making decisions regarding the design of the next generation of hand-held power tools. The process generated good results in terms of creating consumer value.[11]

CRITICAL COUNTERCHAOS CHECKLIST

1. Are we capable of developing product breakthroughs?
2. Can we handle major risks that attempts to develop major breakthroughs are likely to generate?
3. Do we understand that we are a complex system existing in a larger complex system called the market and relationships in these complex systems are nonlinear?
4. Do we have an adequate new product idea evaluation process?
5. How do we successfully develop a futuristic product portfolio?

SUMMARY

As long as the company has products that the market accepts and desires, the company is likely to survive and face market adversities.

In this chapter, product-market opportunities are identified in the form of four scenarios. These vary from simple brand extension to total innovation. Many firms may be working in incremental product development, which is mainly expanding the present activities. However, it is maintained that instead of incremental, discontinuous product development goes in the direction of managing for the future. Thus, managing the present versus the future is identified separately. It is maintained here that companies must have present product portfolios as well as futuristic product portfolios. In both cases, generating product ideas and their realization in terms of becoming full-fledged products are critical.

The chapter details the process of developing a futuristic product portfolio. Futuristic product development is a form of hedging against market adversities.

Finally it is posited that there is also a service portfolio that is consistent with product portfolio development. It is further argued that if these product and service portfolios are congruent, there will be a synergistic impact.

Chapter 9

The Drive to Innovate

In Chapter 8 we had a presentation regarding developing new products and services. It was argued that companies may be managing the present and developing products incrementally or managing the future by radical innovations. The company, hence, may be steadily involved in the development of a current portfolio or a futuristic portfolio. But being steadily involved in a product portfolio may not quite indicate the extent and the force of the company's drive to innovate. The process of innovation as a counterchaos measure goes beyond being steadily involved in a product portfolio. It calls for radical product innovation as quickly and as effectively as possible. Although many companies such as 3M and Motorola have a tradition of innovation, generating radical innovation calls for more than just a tradition. It calls for a *drive* to innovate. Figure 9.1 illustrates the key aspects of such a drive.

CORPORATE CULTURE

As implied earlier in Chapters 6 and 7, all corporations have a culture with a certain value system, orientation, and preference in resource allocation. The corporate culture that supports an aggressive innovation drive has to value innovation above all. In so doing, it not only encourages but also facilitates an innovation orientation. Of course, in order to accomplish these aims, the company manages to allocate substantial resources to this end.

Although it may be ongoing, the drive will be triggered by a perceived market development, which either indicates an immediate risk and/or identifies an unexpected market opportunity. When the invention of wireless cell phones was announced, this event needed to be foreseen as a serious threat for telephonic equipment producers as well as a new opportunity. But without an innovative drive, the reaction to this development could not be swift and effective.

To the extent that the corporate culture perceives the risk and/or the opportunity and reacts proactively, the innovative drive accelerates. Indeed, the corporate culture must be proactive enough so that it will expect sudden chaotic shocks to emerge.

The drive to innovate that is stimulated by the corporate culture, by definition, goes against the *incumbency* status. Traditionally, entry barriers to industries have been connected to sustainable incumbent advantage. However, equipped with the drive to innovate along with powerful aggressiveness, innovative new firms leapfrogged over incumbents and took advantage of market opportunities, while incumbents suffered traditionalism or conventional wisdom.[1] Incumbency typically implies using sustaining technologies;[2] hence, these companies are more engaged in incremental innovation rather than radical innovation. The American automotive manufacturers were experiencing an incumbency status before the Japanese invasion. They were not at all ready for the shock that Japanese competitors brought into the economy. The end result was a loss of about 35 percent of the total automotive market.

IMPROVISATION ONCE AGAIN

The drive to innovate has a special role to play, which is displayed in three distinct features. First, it enhances the firm's agility to cope with unexpected and devastating chaotic market pressures. Because the firm has learned to improvise, it has the agility to respond. Second, improvisation is quite likely to shorten the response time of the firm to unexpected market adversities. If the firm is not proficient in improvisation, it will still respond to the undesirable market conditions, but when it is equipped to do so because of improvisation, the firm will act quickly and quite successfully. Third, the firm, because of improvisation, will be able to bring its innovation to the market speedily, which will give the firm a much more proactive status and perhaps would enhance its market leadership. A mortgage banking company that has been performing well had never entertained the scenario of significantly reduced interest rates. When interest rates started declining seriously in the early 1990s, it did not know what to do. However, a competitor had been using improvisation and was ready for such an event. Whereas the first company got into serious financial problems because of its delayed reaction, the second one performed well under the new and substantially devastating market conditions. To compete in the face of dramatic market changes, firms must create portfolios of innovation that will either extend their existing technical trajectory or move into totally different markets or products. In other words, firms must create innovative streams.

In dealing with the drive to innovate, as discussed in Chapter 8, the critical dichotomy of innovating for the present or for the future emerges as a very serious issue. It stands to reason that the present cannot be ignored or neglected, nor can the future. This may mean that it is wise to develop a present product portfolio as well as a futuristic product portfolio. Such activity is coined as *ambidextrousity*. It has been claimed that small- and medium-sized companies seem to succeed in such endeavors more than large firms. However, the corporate culture must be such that in its efforts to facilitate the drive to innovate, it will establish and support ambidextrousity. This way the firm will successfully create innovative streams.

If the firm is ambidextrous and is creating two types of distinct streams, that is, evolutionary and revolutionary, it must also be prepared and willing to cannibalize some of its existing products.

WILLINGNESS TO CANNIBALIZE

Unfortunately, revolutionary developments via radical innovation are not properly stimulated and supported if the firm does not have a willingness to cannibalize its own products. Cannibalization of the firm's own product goes beyond just the products themselves, but some of the investments through which the products that are to be cannibalized are produced.

Just what kinds of firms think of cannibalization? Grove[3] states: ". . . the person who is the star of a previous era is often the last one to adapt to change." Thus, being a powerful incumbent in the industry is not conducive to cannibalization. Then what? If the firm develops or has a major future market focus, if the up-and-coming radical products have champions in the organization who are pushing these products, if the firm has multiple organizational structures with high internal autonomy and are competing with each other, and if the firm can realize that for a greater future market power, some of the specialized investments need to be abandoned.[4]

Although speed to market has been mentioned a few times in Chapters 7 and 8, it is not quite related to the drive to innovate. But, perhaps this is the key element of counterchaos strategy.

INNOVATIVE SPEED

In Figure 9.1, the last item is the ability to incrementalize or radicalize on short notice. Research posits that competitors fail to respond to radical innovations and to new products that employ a niche strategy.[5] Here it is obvious that if the new products are not recognized within the constraints of the company's existing product category, they may not even be noticed. However, here the discussion must revolve around, not only reactive, but primarily proactive, behavior. The above statement indicates that even as reactive participants, firms are missing their opportunities. However, and above all, here we advocate proactive behavior as the essence of the drive to innovate.

Radically new products, that is, those product innovations that are not quite in line with the existing spectrum of products, create at least two types of uncertainties: first, the uncertainty concerning the expected success of the product and consequences of such an innovation; second, uncertainty concerning the target market. Here, then, when we are talking about short notice, it becomes clear that not only is a revolutionary or evolutionary product brought into focus swiftly, but also it reaches the target market speedily.

Interestingly enough, because of the overwhelming powers of conventional wisdom (mostly negative), competitors may react more readily to market introduction of incremental new products and less readily to radically new products.[6] This is due to the fact that conventional-wisdom-suffering incumbents expect incremental changes in their main activity areas, but they are not equipped to cope with radical innovations coming from competitors. Similarly, an undifferentiated strategy targeting the whole market with the same product and marketing mix creates a wide-scale appeal in general. However, since it does not appeal to a differentiated target market, competitors are not directly influenced and, therefore, their reaction is limited in nature. Competitive reaction to an undifferentiated strategy in such cases would be more limited to the introduction of a new product.

Another consideration regarding the target market is that when a new product, even a radically new product, is introduced in a niche market, because of the specificity of the product and smallness of the target market, it may not get proper attention from competitors. Thus, competitive reaction may be small or negligible, however, if our company is on the receiving end, meaning that it is not introducing that new product but being a competitor. These situations pose a real threat since most companies, including ours, may be ignoring such major potential threats.

Figure 9.1.
The Drive to Innovate.

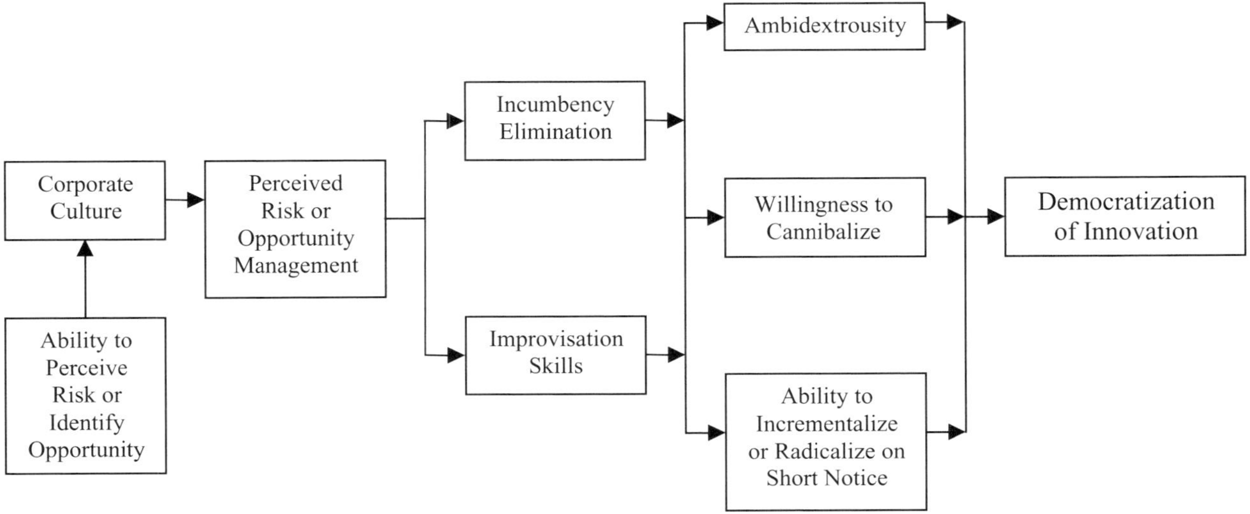

The ability to detect a significant happening or a major change in the market swiftly is part of the last item in Figure 9.1. Making a defensive but preferably offensive move on short notice is, more than partially, detecting the market changes fast.

The mechanics of innovating, discussed in Chapter 8, have only a little to do with this chapter's theme, The Drive to Innovate. All good intentions and activities in routine research and development undertakings do not come close to dealing with the drive, which, this author believes, stems from the corporate culture.

THE ESSENTIALS OF INNOVATIVE BEHAVIOR

The corporate culture, on top of developing futuristic portfolios, having an innovation program, and exercising improvisation, must have the drive, indeed the passion, for innovation. This drive and/or passion for innovation that is a required managerial characteristic can be analyzed in at least seven identifiable functional areas that are listed in Table 9.1.

Taking the First Mover Advantage

Unlike conventional wisdom and its resultant condition of the status of incumbency, the first mover advantage is one of the pivotal forces to be cultivated. The innovative and proactive firm realizes the importance of the first mover advantage. In fact, what is stated somewhat unseriously in many commercials and in common parlance, here is considered to be very critical,

Table 9.1
Essential Points of Innovative Behavior

Innovative Behavior	Specific Benefits
• Taking the First-Mover Advantage • Seeing the Market In-depth • Innovating Disruptive Technologies • Keeping a Watchful Eye on Emerging Niche Markets • Learning to Commit Resources to Product Breakthroughs • Swiftly Reacting to Opportunities and Threats • Always Exploring Latent Needs	• Significant benefits in a short time • Improving potential profits in the long run • Preemptive strength • Managing the present well • Creating potential first-mover advantage • Enhancing survival chances • Managing the future well

that is, "we may not have a second chance to make a first impression." It has been established that the first innovator or the first entrant into the market establishes a great advantage in terms of name recognition and in terms of profits. It has been maintained that pioneers and first movers quite often retain the reward of a large market share long after they have been the first mover.[7] Thus, proper innovative behavior must always be seeking out the first-mover advantage.

See the Market in Depth

Markets are not homogeneous. There are very significant differences regarding preferences, behavior patterns, interests, capabilities, and the like. An innovating firm must pay much attention not only to the market as a whole but particularly to the detail regarding the existing segments. Analyzing the market in depth is essential for future success and for avoidance of the unexpected chaotic market changes. This activity improves potential profits in the long run.

Innovating Disruptive Technologies

Innovative and proactive firms do not rely on sustaining technologies and do not depend on customers and investors for ideas and resources. They are most likely to enter new and small markets and cultivate multiple niches one niche at a time. They foresee markets that do not even exist. They use their own technology over supply to generate radical products and innovate radical technologies.[8]

Keeping A Watchful Eye on Emerging Niche Markets

Moore[9] discusses niche markets as a bowling alley, representing that part of the market in which the new technology is most likely to be adopted. He further maintains that niche markets are to be entered one at a time until the mass market is cultivated. The innovative and proactive firm must always be on the lookout for newly emerging market niches and products, again, to avoid chaos and capitalize on new opportunities.

The management of Schering-Plough, a New Jersey pharmaceutical firm, detected the forthcoming boom in the over-the-counter (OTC) drug market. They based this detection on the following observations: first, prescription drug costs are soaring; second, people are more attracted to lower-cost and less restricting medicines; third, people are more inclined to self-medicate; and fourth, the largest growing sector in our society is the elderly and they are likely to buy disproportionate volumes of OTC products. The company commissioned its product-development teams to generate new OTC products.[10]

Learning to Commit Resources to Product Breakthroughs

As was discussed in Chapter 8, developing and maintaining a futuristic portfolio and cultivating the possibilities of product breakthroughs is a critical part of the innovative dynamics. Samli and Weber[11] posit that breakthroughs are much more costly and risky than developing and introducing simple product line extension. Therefore, breakthroughs need to be managed differently. In such circumstances the aggressive movement toward generating breakthroughs requires a long time and large financial commitments. Behind the whole process is company foresight. This is closely related to the firm's market knowledge and competence. Here if the company is trying to minimize risk, it also minimizes the chances of developing breakthrough products. Thus, company foresight can be translated into serious risk-taking, in other words, foresight goes much beyond developing better quality products in less time for lower costs, which is conventional wisdom and incrementalism, and is depicted also as *new product myopia*. Since such a product is a radical deviation from conventional activity, consumers may have some degree of anxiety due to the newness of the product and perhaps due to prevailing technophobia. Such counterdevelopment forces, by definition, indicate, to some degree, slower acceptance. The higher the technological complexity and newness of the product, the more hesitant consumers are in accepting it. Thus, staying power on the part of the company is critical. If and when there is a radically different product introduced in the market by a competitor, all the attempts to develop on the part of our company become more realistic, and our radically different product becomes more acceptable by the market. Our ability to stay with the breakthrough would enhance our chances of generating a *first-mover advantage* for ourselves (Table 9.1). For instance, the promotion of hybrid cars and their acceptance will play an important role in the acceptance of fuel cell cars. Both are radical innovations, but the fact that one is gaining acceptance creates a rather open mind for the consumer to explore, evaluate, and accept other radical deviations from the conventional technologies.

Swiftly Reacting to Opportunities and Threats

Speed to market has been mentioned a number of times in this book. But in order to facilitate speed to market, first, opportunities and/or treats must be detected and assessed. Again, dwelling upon the statement of we

Table 9.2
Latent Need Exploration

The Key Factors Used To Approximate Latent Needs	Parameters of Latent Demand
What business are we in?	Pinpointing the direction in which our industry and our firm are headed.
What are the areas on which our current customers put more emphasis?	Establishing where the future values are likely to be found.
Will we have the same customers or will they be quite different?	With changing values, new market segments emerge.
What are the current most problematic consumer-related socioeconomic areas?	Choosing the areas where the most contribution could be made.
What are the current most-paid-attention-to societal developments?	Developing a sense of proportionalism.

may not get a second chance to make a first impression, we must be very sensitive to market developments and decisive on the innovational paths we take. The reaction time on the part of the company to, say, a chaotic development, must be minimized. Certainly earlier points of commitment to manpower, financial resources, and staying power all shorten the reaction time and make the company much more resilient. Thus, our firm enhances its chances for survival.

Always Exploring Latent Needs

Latent need exploration is extremely critical for dynamic innovative behavior. After all, if we don't know where we are going, we are not likely to get there. Latent needs exploration is managing the future well. This concept is discussed further in Chapter 10. However, in terms of a general orientation to analyzing latent demand, Table 9.2 is constructed. There are at least five key areas where latent demand characteristics look from the firm's perspectives into societal consumer behaviors. A brief discussion of these five areas is presented.

What Business Are We In?

Although there may be many unrelated areas to explore, it makes more sense to partially limit the latent demand exploration focus primarily to our perception of what business we are in. Here it is necessary to be critically accurate. For instance, McDonald's may not be considered just a hamburger place, but rather a youth entertainment outlet. Certainly, the difference between these two orientations would indicate extremely different latent demand possibilities. Thus, pinpointing the direction of our industry and/or our firm would become more realistic.

Areas of Current Emphasis

Just what are the areas on which our current customers are putting more emphasis? In general terms, are they more into convenience, efficiency, speed, quality, enjoyment, and the like? This would enable the company to identify where the future values are likely to be found.

Same or Different Customers

If we follow our future value analysis, will we be able to maintain our current target markets, or will they be totally and/or partially different? If different, in which direction, and how would this influence their behavior pattern? Here it is reasonable to expect the emergence of new and perhaps unexpected market segments.

What Are the Consumers' Biggest Problems?

If we can determine the most serious problems our customers (or consumers in general) are facing, then we can identify the areas where the most important contributions could be made. This approach would indicate how and why the consumer quality of life is enhanced.

Current Societal Developments

There are always current societal trends. It would be very beneficial to identify and analyze them. Some of these trends will have critical indications regarding latent demands. Here our company can deal with one or more of these according to their assessed importance, and according to both our company's financial and know-how capabilities.

Perhaps one of the biggest areas of concentration is surfaced by Silverstein and Fiske[12] under the umbrella title of *emotional spaces*. A large niche market is emerging in the form of demanding new luxuries. This niche is generated by the fact that consumers nowadays marry later, have fewer children, many get divorced, live alone, and pamper themselves; they have more income, they buy their essential products in discount places such as Costco, BJs, Sam's, and the like and save money so that they can splurge on one or more new luxuries. Thus this group of people in the niche markets has at least four emotional spaces: care of me; connecting to certain others, question in terms of adventure or learning, and individual style of self-expressing or self-branding; these emotional spaces are all futuristic. The chances are that there will be more such emotional spaces. These emotional spaces in these niche markets call for what Silverstein and Fiske[13] coined new luxuries. Retail establishments such as Crate and Barrel, Williams-Sonoma, or Victoria's Secret, have paid attention to the emerging niche markets and their needs. Needless to say, many manufacturers and distributors are involved in this all-powerful activity of emerging niche markets, and are stimulated by thinking outside-the-box orientation. No doubt, much improvisation and drive for creativity underscore this new wave of market opportunities and chaotic forces that would disrupt the conventional, internally stimulated new product, and service development activity of the company.

OUR COMPANY MUST SEE BENEATH THE SURFACE

The dynamic corporate drive to innovate, as our discussion indicates, must see beneath the surface of what is happening. In describing stock market behavior, it has been said that amateurs think that if it is up, it is going to go up farther and if it is down, it will go down further. The dynamic corporate innovative behavior must not fall into such a trap. Here it is necessary to see what is happening beneath the surface. If wholesale clubs or retail supercenters are emerging, that does not necessarily mean that there is a need for more of these. It may mean that another approach that will yield better results may be needed.

Here the disruptive technologies teach a lesson. Certainly they indicate there are other and better ways of solving a problem than simply conventional wisdom. Furthermore, the emergence of new luxuries teaches another lesson. Here improvisation in the form of scenario development can be totally invaluable in generating new and exciting product lines and placing them in the market in the form of *fast fashions*. These fast fashions are an answer to chaotic changes in the market and they present a very important example of how chaotic market changes can be a very significant market opportunity for the proactive firm.

CRITICAL COUNTERCHAOS CHECKLIST

1. What are the characteristics of our corporate culture?
2. Do we suffer from an acute case of incumbency, which implies that we use sustaining technologies and are we very comfortable with this orientation?

3. How do we develop a drive to innovate and make it a critical aspect of our corporate culture?
4. Are we willing to cannibalize some of our products even though they are at least marginally profitable?
5. Do we appreciate the benefits of innovative behavior?

SUMMARY

Perhaps the most important message of this chapter is that opportunities do not happen; they are made. An innovative tradition is not enough. A dynamic innovative behavior is extremely critical. Such dynamic behavior is proactive. It receives its dynamism from the corporate culture. Our firm has (or should have) an uncanny ability to detect new risks and opportunities. Furthermore, our firm is capable of prioritizing such risks and opportunities. By eliminating the tendency to become an incumbent and by cultivating improvisation skills, our firm can develop a highly functional list of opportunities that are carefully prioritized. Here it is argued in this chapter that our firm has to be ambidextrous and, while dealing with the future, not to neglect the present. This means, if needed, our firm cannibalizes its own current products and, at times, incrementalizes innovations as it also radicalizes innovations, both on extremely short notice.

The chapter articulates the essentials of dynamic innovative behavior. Here a seven-point discussion is presented.

Finally, a special section is presented that deals with exploration of latent needs, which happens to be one of the most critical factors on which this book is based. Five critical questions are raised dealing with what kind of business we are in, our customers' current priorities, continuity of our current target markets, what are the most problematic areas our customers are facing, and, finally, what are the key societal trends.

APPENDIX: BEST IDEAS OF 2005 LEADING TO DEVELOPMENT OF FUTURISTIC PRODUCTS

Simplicity: Latest buzz in management and design. Ease of use is critical. The iPod nano nails it. So do Rocio Romero's Spartan, up-in-four-days prefab homes are raised. Jura Capresso has a one-button espresso maker. Things must be stripped down to their basics and make products intuitive.

Biological destiny: Gene contains the instructions for proteins that are building blocks of life. But genes according to *epigenetics* act according to environmental and chemical factors. A sister molecule RNA can control important cell functions and can be manipulated by drugs.

The knowledge economy: Creative economy information is now a commodity. Focus is on new corporate core competencies. In order to prosper, companies change the game in their industries by creating products and services that satisfy needs consumers don't even know they have yet. Mastering new design methods and learning new innovation metrics are keys to corporate success.

Full-blown experience: Instead of better or cheaper products now it is becoming to create wonderful and emotional experiences for consumers around whatever is being sold. It is the experience that counts. Cult brands such as Starbucks or Apple started it but it is becoming the norm. Building communities of passionate and loyal consumers. This is the next step beyond customization of what we make. Umpqua Bank pays admission to a club (The Experience Economy).

Inflation targeting: Target level for future inflation and issue updates to inspire investor confidence and keep market rates stable. It is working in Britain, Sweden, China, and Brazil.

Open source workplace: The best ideas may evolve from the bottom-up and sometimes from the outside-in. Any employee can create, edit, refine, comment on, or fix an idea. From chaos to a path to greater productivity. The workplaces become more transparent as power and information are instantly shared. There may even be virtual commons, such as Procter & Gamble's using the wisdom of online crowds at InnoCentive, a Web network of 80,000 scientists, to find solutions for problems. Peer production creates value.

Pop culture play stations: Video gaming featuring skateboard stars is powerful. Electronic arts have developed the Next Level Music Label to sell music from its games to be used in television commercials and/or ring tones.

Fab fakes and cheap chic mass class: Consumers of all classes buy their catsup at Costco and organic beef at Whole Foods. The poor and the rich both are buying at discount stores and also frequenting technologically forefront companies selling advanced products.

Reaching simultaneous media multitasking consumers: Explosion of technology and choices has pushed media multitasking across the generational divide. Everyone is now a simultaneous consumer of media. They can be reached through "foreground" and "background." A television show that runs at a low hum while people are working on a computer. The podcasts play between telephone calls. Multiple layers of media may play at once. We have more hours of media coming to us than the hours of the day.

Where young people hang out online: MySpace.com is a special networking site. There is no distinction between virtual and physical reality. There are over 300 networking destinations. Cyber community centers are very active. An online social presence is critical to navigating the offline world.

Marching to own music: Ventura clothing lets employees take breaks if the surf is good or if there is fresh snowfall. Weather cannot wait but work can. Capable employees know how to get their work done and can judge the rhythms of their day without constant monitoring. Work-life balance is more productive.

Source: Adopted and revised from "Best Ideas of 2005," *Business Week*, December 19, 2005, 74–81.

Chapter 10

Using One's Strengths

The corporate culture, driven to innovate and aspiring to achieve almost constant peak performance in fulfilling its great mission, must be able to get the most out of its resources, particularly its human resources.

The corporate entity, which happens to be a group of people who got together to accomplish something collectively that they cannot accomplish individually, must know what its strengths and its weaknesses are and must be able to focus on its strengths. This focus, which goes beyond simply making money into inspiring missions, describes the generation of consumer value. There must be inspiration here that goes beyond self-interest into a cause that truly benefits the consumer, in particular, and society as a whole.

THE FOCUS FACTOR

Many years ago Peter Drucker stated that a business enterprise has two key functions: marketing and innovation.[1] However, some half a century later, this author believes that the key function of the modern enterprise is more than those: it is managing the future. For this to be accomplished, the firm must focus on its resources and their use so that it could go where the market is going to be (the Gretzky Principle).

In order to establish some degree of market superiority, the firm must be able to develop competencies to utilize its resources optimally. In order to accomplish this, the firm must be very cognizant of its strengths and must focus on these. Thus, developing, recognizing, and using core competencies are essential for development and use of market power that will protect the firm against chaotic occurrences as they enhance the firm's market superiority.

If the firm is unfocused, like PepsiCo, it may fail to find synergy in its multiple product lines and one of its product lines can undermine others. In the case of PepsiCo the restaurant chains compete with the beverage prospects so they do not create a much-needed synergism.[2]

Although it can be posited that by recognizing its core competencies, a firm can clearly define its organizational boundaries that would identify what it can profitably do and what it cannot, sometimes the situation is perceived as a given. When core competencies are considered as givens, then core competencies can become building blocks to the implementation of corporate strategies. But it must be recognized that core competencies change, indeed in some cases they need to change. When the firm focuses on its necessary core competencies as its future plans change, it becomes inevitable that some of its core competencies need to be modified. Thus, the focus factor must be flexible enough to encompass modified or newly acquired competencies as well.

CORE COMPETENCIES ARE NOT FIXED

Wal-Mart relentlessly focuses on satisfying customer needs. The company's goals were to provide customers access to quality goods and make these goods available when and where customers want them at competitive prices, along with building and maintaining a reputation of high-level trustworthiness. The company replenishes inventory through cross-docking. Here goods are continuously delivered to warehouses, where they are selected, repacked, and dispatched to stores, often without being part of the inventory in the warehouse. Thus, Stalk et al.[3] describe modern competition as not just products and markets, but the dynamic nature of companies' behavior. The behavior here is interpreted into key processes that are identified and made difficult to imitate. Such key processes are based on core competencies, which become strategic capabilities. It is important to see if Wal-Mart can continue with this super-process strategy and not lose focus as did K-Mart.

This type of capability-based competition is vulnerable to new processes introduced unexpectedly by a competitor that would force the company's current core competencies into becoming very serious building blocks. It is difficult for companies, particularly those that are incumbents or traditionalists, to develop a new set of core competencies and dramatically change their key processes and develop new and more powerful

Figure 10.1.
Interaction between Strategic Business Units and Profit Centers.

	High Market Power (SBUs) Low	
High	STARS Using a major portion of the firm's resources (Build)	CASH COWS Using only a small portion of resources (Hold)
Low	QUESTION MARKS Use limited resources (Harvest)	DOGS Use (if any) very limited amount of resources (Divest)

(Left axis label: Profit Power (PCs))

Source: Adapted and revised from Samli and Shaw (2002).

capability-based competitiveness. The competitiveness of the firm, at least partially, is reflected in the performance of its profit centers and strategic business units.

RELATIONSHIP BETWEEN PROFIT CENTERS AND STRATEGIC BUSINESS UNITS

All firms operate as if they are composed of multiple businesses. Johnson and Johnson, for instance, has many products, and each is almost like a separate business. Some of these products provide and enhance market power for the company. This outreach for the firm is made possible by its strategic business units (SBUs). In the case of Johnson and Johnson, baby powder or band-aids and other consumer products have enhanced the company's name. In other words, one can say they acted as strategic business units (SBUs) so that the company's profit centers (PCs) would generate greater returns to investments. Levi's blue jeans is another example of SBU. The company reaches out to the market with its jeans but in the stores there are many more profitable and attractive designer jeans (PCs) that generate more income. Thus, the company's market power (SBUs) brings more profit activity (PCs). These two aspects of the business, any business, if balanced, would optimize the firm's performance in the marketplace.

Figure 10.1 illustrates the optimality of the balance between SBUs and PCs. As can be seen, horizontally the strength of SBUs is observed, and vertically, PCs are evaluated. The firm has true stars as shown in the upper left quadrant. These stars require a major portion of the firm's resources to be enhanced further. Similarly, the lower right quadrant deals with "dogs" that need to be eliminated. Question marks can be futuristic and deserve some serious attention. However, as was discussed earlier, if the question marks represent part (or all) of a futuristic portfolio, the decision needs to be made as to how much attention should be given to the future and how much attention to the present. One point is rather clear here, that is, the cash cows do not have much future, but they are financing the present and future by yielding revenues that are not expected to last too long. Thus the company is competing both in the present and the future by using its capabilities. Once again, the dynamics of its behavior is making the company succeed in putting together a strong market power and profit power. Here the firm is recognizing its core competencies, which enable it to clearly define its capabilities and weaknesses. By doing so, the firm makes it possible to focus its resources for optimal advantage.[4]

Snyder and Ebeling[5] take the following position: "Identifying core competencies and inspiring the organization to nurture and organize around them is one of the most important contributions senior management can make." However, here the senior management is trying to develop the strategic intent of the company to identify, nurture, and organize around activities that are unique and enduring and would enhance its abilities to generate consumer satisfaction. Top management's orientation makes a critical difference. Whether top management is convention-bound or futuristic determines the nature of core competencies. The attempts to identify core competencies based on conventional wisdom versus proactive, counterchaos orientation are most likely to generate dramatically different results. It must be realized that misidentified core competencies can become core inhibitors or roadblocks to success. And, of course, followers in great organizations such as Ciba-Geigy or Hewlett-Packard receive their strengths from the vision of the leaders who are more futuristic than conventional.

"CONVENTIONAL" VERSUS "PROACTIVE" DICHOTOMY

In Chapters 2 and 3, discussions are introduced dealing with the problem of conventional wisdom. If the leaders of the organization are very conventional or very proactive, how would such a dichotomy play out in identifying the core competencies of the company?

When Levitt discussed marketing myopia, among other examples, he described the difficulties that the motion picture industry has encountered with the introduction and enhanced popularity of TVs in our society. In order to illustrate the conventional and proactive dichotomy, the following discussion hypothetically distinguishes the top executives of the participants in the motion picture industry. It must be reiterated that the

Table 10.1
Strategic Planning in Support of Innovative Developments

Conventional Orientation	Proactive Counterchaos Orientation
Strategic planning as continuation of the past	Strategic planning in support of revolutionary innovation
Market research to justify decisions	Market research to explore new opportunities
Benchmarking based on industry's past performance	Benchmarking outside the particular industry
Competitive analysis to follow industry leaders	Analysis to explore new areas of leadership
Establishing the parameters about what we are doing	Establishing the parameters about what we are not doing
Strategic plan as an annual ritual	Strategic plan as an unfinished product
Strategy as the domain of executive elite	Democratization of the strategic plan
Attention largely to financial health	Attention largely to market performance and strategic plan

Source: Adapted and revised from Turock (2002).

industry did come out of a very troubled era. But it could have done much better if the corporate dynamics were to go beyond the conventional thinking and reconsider the core competency areas. The following discussion is based on the eight top management considerations that play such a big role in identifying and implementing the company's strategic dynamics. These eight considerations are illustrated in Table 10.1.

If the industry had taken strategic planning as a continuation of the past, it would have said (and indeed at the beginning of the problem it did): "Our core competency is being creative on the silver screen and making movies." If its strategic planning were to be more supportive of revolutionary innovations, the industry would have decided that its core competency was to provide entertainment for the masses.

In conventional wisdom, orientation market research is used to justify or confirm decisions. Here, again, core competency may have been defined as making good movies. However, proactive orientation research would explore new opportunities. In this case, core competency could have been defined as working with the television industry and jointly developing better entertainment opportunities.

Benchmarking or identifying the best practices under the conventional orientation would have meant the practices of the best studios that are producing movies and therefore, core competencies would be based on these practices. In proactive orientation, benchmarking would have been based on the practices that prevail in the most proactive and creative industries. These practices would determine the core competencies.

Competitive analysis would assess and perhaps improve upon the leaders' practices in the industry. Again, this would have been following what the major motion picture studios practice and, again, identifying the core competencies accordingly. Proactive practices analysis would have been to explore new areas of leadership based on the trends and latent needs. Core competencies, in this case, would have been concentrating on, say, the national TV networks and establishing core competencies accordingly.

In conventional wisdom orientation, establishing the parameters of what the company is all about is a standard orientation. Again, it may have been that, at the beginning, motion picture studios established the parameters of what they are and what they do based on a very narrow version of making movies, short features, and cartoons. Hence the core competencies were established accordingly. However, in proactive orientation, parameters need to be established not on what the company and the industry are doing but on what the company and the industry are not doing. It would have been such that the motion picture industry could have assessed its impact on the society and explored how it could have been more influential and created better and more captivating entertainment. Core competencies would have been identified much more differently from what they had been at that time.

Under conventional wisdom, the strategic plan has been treated as an annual ritual. The motion picture studios might have identified the types of movies they planned on producing during the planning period and might have identified the promotional activity for these movies. In proactive orientation, however, the strategic plan is looked at as an unfinished product. Studios would have asked themselves: "How do we improve the public entertainment?" and "So what is next?"

Conventional orientation always has the tendency to treat strategy as the domain of the executive elite. The motion picture industry, at the outset, probably did not treat strategy any differently. However, democratization of the strategic plan, that is, sharing it with the company employees, as advocated by the proactive orientation, is likely to create much inside support as well as generating new internal ideas for the strategic plan and its implementation.

Finally, particularly during the early era of the motion picture industry, conventional orientation put almost all of its attention on the company's financial health. Thus, the industry at the beginning may not have seen television as an emerging danger. In proactive orientation, attention is given largely to market performance and the strategic plan. The motion picture industry would have reacted much sooner to the challenge of the television industry if it had exercised a more proactive orientation. The difference between the conventional and proactive orientations, thus, not only have a very significant impact on identifying and exercising the core competencies, but also on developing and enhancing market power.

UNDERSTANDING THE MARKET POWER

Moore[6] describes market power as a firm's entering the mainstream market and getting out of a niche market. This is, of course, if the niche market becomes a major part of the mainstream market. He identifies the market power in such cases as adjunct, rather than nil, because at this point our company is not a key player, just a protégé of the niche market we are coming from. With an increasing presence in the marketplace, market power establishes market leadership, which partially occupies a preferred and privileged position. These features translate into market power. This may mean to charge more for the same product even if the product may not be quite bug-free. Intel Pentium was sold at a price about 33 percent higher than a bug-free product by NexGen. This is perhaps because Intel was the market leader and commanded greater name recognition, customer confidence, and volume sold. Because of the volume, the market leader achieves economies of scale, lowering the cost per unit produced and shipped. Moreover, because of the name recognition, the market leader does not try as hard to sell as the newcomers.

MARKET POWER AND PROFIT CENTERS

The market power of the leadership position, however, in time can create an incumbency status, and the firm becomes vulnerable to new and radical innovations, disruptive technologies, and other chaotic influences. If unprepared and without the necessary corporate culture, the firm will be as vulnerable in entering other markets and/or concentrating on other products and services.

Thus, even though market power yields a privileged position keeping a firm reasonably immune to chaotic changes, at the same time, it can also create an unfortunate situation whereby the firm neglects to become proactive, and thus suffers through an incumbency syndrome. The firm's market power is reinforced by its strategic business units and, subsequently, its profit centers. In a dynamic market system, not only the relative market power of SBUs may change, but also SBUs may change places with PCs or vice-versa. In other words, a profit center may become a strategic business unit, or a strategic business unit may become a profit center. Levi's blue jeans were at one point a major profit center for the company. However, in recent years, the company has been thinking of dropping blue jeans because they are not yielding enough profit, although using the blue jeans (rather than dropping them) as a strategic business unit is likely to be a good decision for the company. Standard blue jeans by Levi's at this point can be considered an SBU, since the company is known by this flagship product. Although it may not be as profitable as more fashionable lines of the company (PCs), it helps the company to have a strong market presence.

It must be reiterated that SBUs and PCs are intimately connected to the firm's market power. And, as such, they must be identified and recognized accordingly.

As an illustration, consider the following:

A corner drugstore in a major Southeast university town has always had a very active lunch hour. One day the lunch customers found the lunch counter closed. The explanation by the management was that the lunch counter was not yielding profit. However, the management had not studied the in-store purchases of lunch customers. They were buying many things in the store before or after lunch. The drugstore did not distinguish its lunch counter as SBU that generated much business within the store. SBUs do not have to be very profitable themselves to generate profit through PCs, by bringing the customers to the drugstore. Here the strategic business unit is almost part of the overall promotional efforts of the business.

HOW DOES THE COMMUNICATION MIX WORK?

The market system is a complex communications network. Considering the fact that no business can be successful in the marketplace as a well-kept secret, it is important for a firm, any firm, to participate in that complex communication network. Establishing market power is, at least partially, related to name recognition. Be it the name of the firm or its brands, it is critical to realize that if those names are not recognized, the firm is not gaining market power.

Market leaders are not born; they are made. In the making and maintaining leadership, the promotional activity must be taken very seriously. Thus, promotion is deliberate action to establish market leadership by effectively

Table 10.2
Promotional Aspects of A New Product Introduction

- Appealing to our target market with our innovative product to solve some of their up-to-now unsolvable problems.
- Appealing to our target market with our far-out product to solve the problem that they did not know existed.
- The problem is inherent in the current industrial paradigm and is widespread.
- The problem can be solved with our innovative product or service because we are helping the end users by showing how it is done.
- Showing our end users how well we know their problems because we studied them carefully and can prove that we have the answer.
- By cultivating the product's effectiveness and by personalizing its use, we can overcome the initial resistance by the target market toward a new product or service.

Source: Adapted and revised from Moore (1995).

influencing the communication network that prevails in the market. As such, promotion is an investment and not an expense item.

Establishing market leadership and employing the promotion mix to achieve this goal is not a simple task. Table 10.2 illustrates how all the elements of promotion, that is, advertising, personal selling, sales promotion, and public relations, must be used toward a specific end. Here first and foremost advertising and personal selling are not substitutes, but complementary activities. Without advertising, the sales force will have difficulty being accepted. But without personal selling, products cannot reach the market, particularly those involving high-tech.

The general message of Table 10.2 is that we have done our homework and we know your problems in detail. In fact, we even know the problems that you didn't know existed. So let us show how our product can be used to solve your age-old problem or the problems you don't know about. This is a sound orientation and can be used for all products of our company. The end users are likely to react positively to a radically new product if it is presented within an existing product category and offers an unambiguous attack on a prevailing problem or a problem just discovered by us. The greatest danger here is to claim more than what we are capable of delivering. In the market system, unfortunately, bad new spreads much faster than good news. Thus, in our efforts to establish and enhance market power, we must be factual, correct, and display real affinity to the needs and feelings of the end users. The selling style is likely to be consultative in the sense that the direct sales force will advise the prospective buyers, and in so doing, it will differentiate our company by providing expertise for that particular segment. This effort is backed up with advertising and direct communication with knowledge workers, the think tank of the company. The think tank can be particularly effective in helping the sales people to solve the unique problems of specific prospects.

Assuming the existence of a proactive management orientation, all the attempts and efforts toward generating market power, can, at least for a short while, isolate and perhaps protect the firm from unexpected chaotic influences. By the same token, they would facilitate speed to market and swift responses that are carried out to the target markets. If, for instance, the firm has established itself as a leader and responds to a disruptive technological development with a new process or a product, the process or the product will be more readily and swiftly accepted by the market.

OUR NAME RECOGNITION IS PRICELESS

It can be speculated that a fuel cell car introduced by Toyota is likely to gain widespread acceptance more swiftly than one that is introduced by, say, Yugo. Name recognition that is the outcome of established market power, can be extremely valuable for proactive marketing, which otherwise can be counterchaotic. Again, it may be reasonable to expect that IBM will introduce the new nanotechnology products. And it is similarly reasonable that these products will be accepted at least partially because of the name recognition. However, it must be reiterated that IBM will have to be willing to cannibalize some of its existing products. Making room for the better product may be costly and painful, but must be done if we want to survive chaotic markets.

Using our strengths and developing them further is clearly related to market power, which may call for making major changes if and when needed, even at the most inconvenient and unexpected times. However, it has been claimed that managers do not really like changes because changes bring about confusion, uncertainty, and even disorder. Being ready to bring about major changes is what this book is about. It is posited that putting our best foot forward and using our strengths optimally necessitates proactive management. When it was agreed upon that the price and performance characteristics of microprocessor-based PCs were extremely powerful, NCR and Hewlett-Packard modified their strategies swiftly and significantly so that they could take advantage of microprocessors while others ignored them.[7]

CHANGEABLE ECONOMIES AND CHANGEABLE STRATEGIES

Economic conditions in markets change. Certainly we cannot control these changes. The only countervailing power we have is our strategic posture. This posture is expressed by our SBUs and PCs. However, if our SBUs and PCs don't change to respond to the market's, occasionally extremely harsh changes, then there is simply no hope for survival. Thus, understanding, identifying, and prioritizing our SBUs and PCs are extremely critical activities for managers. As mentioned earlier, they change and at times reverse roles. The management of the firm needs to take advantage of this dichotomy, since all of our activities and all of our products do not yield high levels of profit nor do they equally function toward generating market power. Using our ability to use SBUs and PCs to optimal advantage, we must follow their performances separately from each other, and we must prioritize them by evaluating their performances. Thus, if the current SBU appears to be not as powerful in 6 months, the management may have to make a decision regarding keeping it as an SBU or deciding on another one. This is similar to IBM's using mainframes as an SBU and subsequently switching to personal computers.[8]

CRITICAL COUNTERCHAOS CHECKLIST

1. Do we have appropriate human resources?
2. Have we developed competencies to utilize our resources optimally?
3. Do we realize that core competencies are not fixed and likely to change as the market conditions and our firm's strategic posture change?
4. Do we know the difference between our strategic business units and profit centers? Can we tell which is which in our corporate entity?
5. Do we treat our strategic plan as an ongoing annual ritual or as an unfinished product?

SUMMARY

Using a company's strengths is not automatic. The firm must focus on what it can do the best, and by using that performance, it must develop market power, perhaps leading to market leadership. The firm's market power is related to its profit power. If its market power gains momentum, it is quite likely that its profitability also will be enhanced.

Using the company's strengths, however, is related to whether the management of the company has a conventional or a proactive orientation. A case is made in this chapter for a proactive orientation. It is maintained that if the management is conventional, the firm will not be able to generate adequate market power. Generating market power and perhaps subsequently becoming a market leader, at least partially and for a period of time, may help the firm to avoid or to counteract chaotic market influences. The firm can use its capabilities fully by identifying its core competencies. However, the core competencies in time may become obsolete and make the firm vulnerable. In establishing market power, the firm must be able to differentiate its strategic business units that create market power. Similarly, the firm must be able to identify its profit centers that would indicate its profit power. These two must be carefully followed and examined, since they change in a dynamic market.

Finally, a brief discussion is presented in the chapter regarding the firm's promotional mix. The more recognized the company name, again at least for a short while, the more likely the firm will be able to cope with unexpected market adversities.

Chapter 11

Because We Have Been Doing It This Way Traditionally

Invariably, all companies have a culture. Whether it is formally constructed and reinforced throughout the company, or informally evolved and implicitly spread out within the corporate entity, culture establishes important parameters of what is acceptable by the company and what is not. Hence, culture teaches employees what the company values are and is a major determinant that shapes the behavior and performance of the company's employees.[1] Powerful and all-encompassing corporate cultures create strong traditions that in time become a big hindrance to progress. As discussed in Chapter 2, in time companies start suffering from active inertia, which, in essence means company traditions become dysfunctional dogmas.[2]

INERTIA TRAPS

Because of their extraordinary importance that would make a firm survive and succeed or fall into blind and total rigid values, a discussion of inertia traps is extremely critical. Table 11.1 illustrates five inertia trap types that can prove to be deadly for the firm in a very dynamic and indeed unfriendly market system. All companies have a success formula that is good to know but never be enslaved by. The five traps are as follows.

Strategic Frames

Sooner or later the firm can develop obsessions of some type. The great A&P grocery chain believed in being number one. This obsession limited

Table 11.1
Recurring Inertia Traps

Inertia Trap Type	The Key Diagnostic Symptoms
Strategic Frames Should Not Be Blinding	Obsessions on some criterion: • We are number one • We beat our competition cold • We are a great company
Resources Cannot Be Dead Weight	Blind loyalty to resources: • Our number one brand brought us here • Our technology is what we work for • The suppliers we use are the best
Processes Are Not Routines	Overwhelmed with good processes of the past: • Read the handbook, it is our Bible • We hire certain types of people and we promote them • We must wait until everybody agrees
Relationships Here Today Gone Tomorrow	Tied to past relationships: • We always used XYZ value chain • Our management people can handle all important problems • We owe it to ABC Enterprises
Values Are Not To Be Dogmas	Abiding by old values as if they cannot be changed: • We are a team and must stay that way • We believe in products that bring in more than X percent of profit • We think of our competitors as mortal enemies

Source: Adapted and revised from Sull (2005).

their profitability and caused detriment for the company. Compaq did not see anybody but IBM as its competitor. But Dell created devastation for the company. Sears appeared to be extremely impressed with its performance and position in merchandising. The company assumed its position was guaranteed and started exploring other ventures such as finance, which proved to be disastrous.

Resources

The company in time can become blindly loyal to resources. Ford Model T may have brought the company to a desirable stage but many other Ford products carried the company out to modern times. Xerox protected its photocopier technology and dismissed simpler technologies. Overwhelming attachment to certain suppliers made it impossible to explore better arrangements.

Processes

Companies can become overwhelmed with good processes of the past. Managers in time have a tendency to make rigid routines out of good processes of the past. From hiring and promoting new talent to updating the product features, not old processes but the new technologies and market needs are what count.

Relationships

All firms have multiple relationships in receiving supplies, getting technological input, developing better products and the like. But becoming tied down to these relationships can be deadly. Compaq, for instance, relied heavily on a value chain it created. But as the market competition changed the company's value chain did not perform well.

Values

Certain clichés in time, which may have reflected corporate values early on in time, can become dogmas and cannot be changed. These tie the company to certain impractical value-triggered behaviors. For a long time Levis did not make critical changes in its strategic decisions to protect its people and plants almost blindly.

It must be realized that inertia traps are beyond conventional wisdom, which is discussed in Chapter 3. These traps can be based on very modern wisdom and can truly become traps in a very fast manner in a fast-changing market environment.

Dell is the world's largest PC maker but at the point of writing this book it may be suffering from inertia traps. These traps are revolving around the four key assumptions that have been guiding the company's practices. They are:

1. Direct will dominate: selling directly to customers, is and has remained the key. But the more complex the products the more consumers are beginning to frequent retail establishments.
2. Association with major tech-giants works. The company has had very tight partnerships with Microsoft and Intel. But these two giants are losing their market power.

3. Commoditization is king. The company does not put emphasis on R&D, it believes in plain-Jane PCs and their large volume distribution. But the R&D activity in the industry can jeopardize Dell's market position.
4. Cost cutting is the winning factor. Winning with cost-cutting based on ruthless efficiency to underprice rivals has been working so far but with possible disruptive technologies emerging from competitors' R&D efforts can put the company in a very vulnerable position.[3]

TRADITIONS DO NOT HAVE A RIGHTFUL PLACE IN FACING CHAOS

Whether it may be coined internal equilibrium or the path of least resistance, companies with strong corporate cultures may develop traditions and hence also create rigidities that may make the company vulnerable to unexpected chaotic market changes.

There are two key factors that are promoted by the corporate culture and directly impact the firm's success. The first is vision, which is the strategic component, and the second is the values that are the behavioral component. Clearly, while the vision statement is geared to answer such questions as to what we expect to accomplish, the value statement would indicate how the whole corporate entity is expected to behave. Companies such as Nokia believe that the value statement is the true driver of the company. Its four core values are rather far-reaching:

• Satisfying customers—by understanding their needs and giving them the best possible value.
• Respecting the individual—valuing people as individuals regardless if they are employees, customers, or business partners.
• Striving for achievement—the company employees are familiar with the company's goals and they are courageous, innovative, and willing to learn.
• Learning continuously—everyone in the company is given a chance to improve themselves and their performance. Everyone in the company keeps an open mind and tries to learn new developments.[4]

If these values lead in a futuristic fashion and translate into action, then the company is quite well-prepared for future shocks. It can swiftly react to unexpected chaotic events and can convert the chaotic events into profitable propositions. In other words, values support and further cultivate the vision. However, these four core values do not necessarily represent a culture of discipline. If and when a company develops a discipline and shared thoughts that lead systematically to proactive thoughts and more futuristic action, then there may be a culture of discipline.[5]

Figure 11.1.
Corporate Culture and Its Outreach.

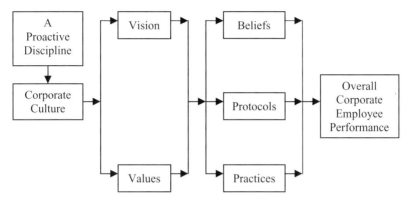

Figure 11.1 illustrates that the corporate culture reaches throughout the corporate entity through instilled beliefs, formally established protocols, and all kinds of practices within the entire corporate entity. Thus, the corporate culture has a profound impact on the company's performance.

However, once the corporate values are established, two separate happenings take place: first, value integration; and second, value credibility. Value integration is considered to be the comprehensive process starting with identifying the company's core values and continuing with the communication and reinforcement of these values. This is how company credos are born. Value credibility is the success of a company in managing its performance according to the values and beliefs that it purports.[6]

It is difficult to claim that the values that are integrated are credible. It is maintained here that many companies with much history and known credo may start considering this whole value system as a powerful tradition, and may start living in the past. It is essential that those values that are integrated remain credible in terms of their worthiness. Their worth stems from their being directly related to their relevancies. Stated simply, well-known historic stances and credos in time lose their relevancies. They become dead weight to the company on the road to progress.

WHEN DISRUPTIVE TECHNOLOGIES ARE EMERGING, TRADITIONS MUST DIE

Living in the glory of the past does not enable the firm to be futuristic enough to manage disruptive technologies used by competitors or economic slowdowns that emerge at very inopportune times. In view of the dynamics and adversities prevailing in markets, the only traditions companies can afford to have are being futuristic and proactive. A simple example may suffice. Many years ago, ABC was a bookkeeping firm. The company had very well trained bookkeepers who were very good in what they did. Furthermore, the company promoted quality service for customers, and each individual in the company would provide the best possible service in the area of bookkeeping. But, when computers emerged and bookkeeping became computerized, there was no longer demand for ABC's services. If ABC was not prepared to give its people detailed crash courses on computers, and if its people were not prepared to make dramatic changes in their work, there would be no future for the company. Bookkeeping as a profession disappeared. Thus, the credibility of the values needs to be assessed and, indeed, even changed, if the survival of the firm is at stake.

Traditions, however good they may sound, should be allowed to die if and when they become counterproductive. Here particularly the words "if" and "when" have particular meaning. If the company does not realize that its long-established traditions are no longer productive and does not move in the direction of changing the traditions swiftly, then the chances for survival in adverse market conditions become very slim.

LEAN THINKING AS AN EXAMPLE OF QUESTIONABLE TRADITION

Lean thinking or being cost-conscious is as important as apple pie or the American flag in business circles. Womack and Jones state:[7]

After a decade of downsizing and reengineering, most companies in North America, Europe and Japan are still stuck, searching for a formula for sustainable growth and success. The problem . . . is that managers have lost sight of value for the customer and how to create it. By focusing on their existing organizations and outdated definitions of value, managers create waste, and the economies of the advanced countries continue to stagnate.

What's needed indeed is lean thinking to help managers clearly specify value, to line up all the value-creating activities for a specific product along a value stream, and to make value flow smoothly at the pull of the customer in pursuit of perfection.

Starting in the early 1980s, special emphasis has been given to the "bottom line." Lean thinking is one of the outcomes of this emphasis. However, this author believes that lean thinking and the special emphasis on the bottom line have led to a rather problematic and questionable stance of managing for a bottom line versus managing by a bottom line. This is the distinction between *market*-oriented or *finance*-oriented. Indeed, profits can be maximized by maximizing the sales volume for a given cost level, the market orientation, or by minimizing the cost for a given sales volume, which is financial management. Although both approaches in the short run aim at the same results, they part company in the long run.

Lean thinking is a very important aspect of finance orientation that is associated with managing by a bottom line, but not managing for a bottom line.[8] Indeed, many companies such as Pratt and Whitney, Porsche, and Toyota have developed a lean thinking tradition.

First, the difference between managing by a bottom line versus managing for a bottom line is that finance-driven businesses typically establish certain financial goals upfront, such as cutting advertising costs by 10 percent or distribution costs by 15 percent and the like. Contrariwise, managing for a bottom line will indicate whatever needs to be done, including increasing costs and expenditures, to reach a profit goal.

It is ironic to realize that while the economy is *market-driven*, many companies are finance-driven and go for cost-cutting and short-run orientations.[9] The problem is that as companies develop a credo (or a tradition) of cost-cutting, they cannot maintain a proactive stance in the marketplace. For instance, downsizing has become a widespread practice since about the 1980s, which has been one of the practices related to cost cutting or lean thinking that has created many problems for corporate entities. While laying off people is done by the personnel division, some of the core competencies of the company decided upon by the strategy division have become depleted, since these two functions, that is, strategy and human resources, are not necessarily on the same wavelength.

Thus, lean thinking and cost cutting can go to extremes and may not generate value for the consumer and profit for the company. But, above all, if lean thinking supersedes a company's other outreach activities, the company becomes incumbent and vulnerable to unexpected market changes. This point is illustrated in Table 11.2. Conventional lean thinking is likely to assume that market demand and industry behaviors are all stable and can easily be predicted. Proactive lean thinking, however, would indicate that both markets and industries, and the demand companies are facing are changing. Such changes are not only difficult to predict but, if neglected, may be creating turbulence or chaos.

Conventional lean thinking assumes that customers' or consumers' behavior is rational; therefore, it can be assumed constant as cost factors are reduced. On the other hand, proactive lean thinking would not count on such a rationality and, hence, if costs are needed to be reduced, they should not influence consumer and/or customer behaviors.

Table 11.2
Differences in Lean Thinking

Conventional Lean Thinking	Proactive Lean Thinking
• Market demand and industries are primarily stable and predictable.	• Market demand and industries are changing fast and creating turbulence or chaos.
• Customers' and consumers' behavior is rational.	• Customers' behavior is somewhat rational and consumers' rationality is highly unlikely.
• Customer value criteria are clear, consistent, and well known. They can be measured and are stable over time.	• Customer value criteria are not clear, inconsistent, and virtually unknown. They can hardly be measured and change in time radically.
• What we can measure is important and sufficient.	• What we can measure is inadequate. There is a measurability gap.
• We can transcend company boundaries to link suppliers, distributors, and customers into an efficient supply chain.	• Such collaboration is not a substitute for competition as driver.
• Lean thinking will always be beneficial to consumers.	• Lean thinking may overshadow other attempts to make the company's efforts more efficient and effective.

Conventional lean thinking assumes the customer value criteria are clear, not changing and well known, so that they can remain stable and be measured accurately over time. Proactive lean thinking assumes just the opposite. Customer value criteria are not clear, they are not consistent, and they are simply not well known. Such unknown entities cannot be measured accurately and are likely to change radically in time.

Again, conventional lean thinking assumes that whatever can be measured about the market and the consumer is important and sufficient. The proactive counterpart, however, believes that whatever is measured about the market and the consumer is certainly important but not at all sufficient. In fact, what we can measure is inadequate and not even reliable. There is a measurability gap in that what we measure is not likely to reflect the total picture.

Conventional lean thinking believes that the company boundaries can be transcended to link with suppliers, distributors, and customers into an efficient supply chain. Proactive lean thinking, on the other hand, would maintain that although such collaboration is quite desirable, it is not a substitute for the healthy competitive behavior of providing better products and services to carefully identified target markets.

Finally, conventional lean thinking advocates that lean thinking is always beneficial to consumers. A proactive lean thinker maintains that although lean thinking is critical, it must not overshadow or dominate other company efforts to become more efficient and effective in the marketplace.

The reason for our discussion regarding lean thinking is that when such a position in the corporate entity becomes a *credo*, it becomes overbearing and interferes with many other corporate activities that will call for spending more money for better returns. Credos or traditions, in time, become a major burden rather than competitive strategic tools. The key point that might be arrived at from Table 11.2 is that the conventional lean thinking type of credo would encourage management by a bottom line rather than managing for a bottom line, indicating that aggressive marketing activity such as increasing promotional activity will not be encouraged or supported. An example may explain: ABC stands for activity-based costing. This is a recent concept that is frequently used in logistics circles. It primarily implies identifying activities based on the inventory or production plans and costing out accordingly. Therein lies a problem. Activities of the past or the immediate past may not indicate what is likely to happen in the near future. Due to some drastic market changes, consumer demands may become very different than previous periods, calling for a completely different set of activities. However, ABC is likely to be based on conventional lean thinking; hence, the company cannot accommodate the changes in the market, nor would it have the agility to protect itself.

PLANS FOR LEARNING VERSUS PLANS TO CONTINUE

"Around here this is the way we do it" is a phrase that spells danger for the corporate entity. Indeed some standard procedures and some basic values are important for the corporate entity to function, but traditions such as lean thinking in a conventional manner can become a major hurdle, and the firm may pay for it dearly by not being able to take advantage of market changes and by compromising its agility to cope with chaotic market changes.

It is important to realize that the discussion could go in the direction of being market-driven versus being a market-driver. As the prevailing thinking of "around here this is the way we always have done it" dominates, as it did in Sears and K-Mart for many years. In essence it continues to dominate. At best the companies were market driven.

Figure 11.2.
Business As Usual versus Futuristic Orientation.

	High Level of Incumbency Low	
Historical	Danger zone in turbulent environment, business as usual orientation.	Safe present, dangerous future, mostly dealing incrementalism.
Orientation		
Proactive	Possible emergence of radical products with overwhelmingly plenty and changing existing products vulnerable, no room for error.	Futuristic, innovative, resilient, emphasizing radical development and long-range survival.

However, if we compare the orientations of Sears and K-Mart with, say, the orientation of Crate and Barrel or Williams-Sonoma stores, which put emphasis on learning and unearthing or discovering the latent needs of the market, we realize that these two chains emerged as market drivers. Both Crate and Barrel, and Williams-Sonoma stores appeared to be futuristic, innovative, and resilient, emphasizing radical development and long-range survival; in short by thinking and acting outside the box achieved wonderful results in the chaotic markets,[10] where K-Mart and Sears have performed rather questionably. If and when the possibilities are there the firm can opt to be a market-driver and plans to learn more rather than just planning to continue. Being a market-driver is a very powerful orientation to succeed in the chaotic markets of the 21st century.

In Chapter 6, a discussion is presented about learning organizations. In addition to the corporate culture, developing a learning organization is a significant deviation from the "we have been doing it this way traditionally" orientation.

As seen in Table 11.2, if the company uses a proactive approach, it will make plans for and put extra emphasis on learning rather than being satisfied with a "business as usual" orientation to research and decision-making. Thus, elimination of incumbency status and getting away from a historical or "business as usual" orientation is essential for establishing and expanding a gainful presence in the marketplace. Figure 11.2 describes this situation. As can be seen, in the upper left-hand quadrant, the danger zone is depicted. Here the firm has a very high level of incumbency in terms of "business as usual," but such behavior is reinforced with historic orientation on the part of the firm in terms of "this is how we have been doing it around here traditionally." This is a dangerous stance that comes automatically as decision-makers choose paths of least resistance with traditional procedures. In the lower right-hand quadrant of Figure 11.2, the ideal situation is depicted. Here the firm is cognizant of its incumbency status and keeps it to a minimum, whereas the total orientation is proactive. The firm can be described as resilient, innovative, and futuristic and hence, it is emphasizing its long-range survival in adverse market conditions. If the firm is proactive but still suffering from a high level of incumbency, then it is highly vulnerable and has little room for error, as seen in the lower left quadrant. Finally, if the firm has a historical orientation but low incumbency practices, it may have a safe present, but its future is rather doubtful, as seen in upper right quadrant.

If the firm wants to get away from being ruled by a large variety of traditions that have become a very rigid credo, it will have to learn how to deal with emerging markets, in addition to changing the corporate culture and developing a futuristic orientation.

In Chapter 2, the *Gretzky Rule* is presented, which posits that going where the puck is likely to be is the key to success. In Chapter 9 we discussed staying on top of megatrends as progressive behavior. We need to take a closer look at emerging markets.

HOW DO WE DISCOVER NEW EMERGING MARKETS?

Just how do emerging markets come into being? Figure 11.3 presents five key forces that may lead to the emergence of new markets. A brief discussion of these is presented as follows.

Emerging Socioeconomic Groups

In time, for numerous reasons, certain socioeconomic groups emerge as niche markets and grow even bigger. Generation X is one of our more recent experiences. Generation Xers are well-educated, environmentally sensitive people who are in their late twenties or early thirties and are still living with their parents and working only part-time. Estimated to be in the millions, during the 1990s this group played an important role in recycling waste into new products. There have even been fashion shows of apparel made out of waste materials.

Latent Needs

As discussed earlier, although it may be difficult to identify these needs, they certainly exist. Sooner or later, they will emerge and create markets for numerous products that we never imagined in the past.

Figure 11.3.
Emerging New Markets.

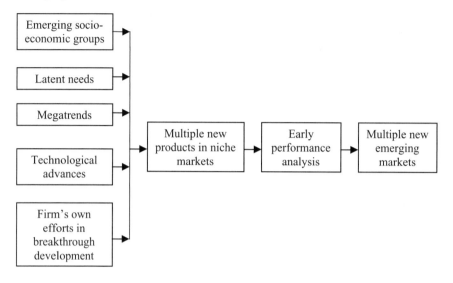

Megatrends

Megatrends are a very important factor in identifying emerging markets. Since this topic is discussed in Chapter 9, it is not analyzed in detail here. However, it is important to indicate that there are always megatrends in the making, and it is critical to track them down and identify their implications for our business.

Technological Advances

Whether they come in the form of disruptive technologies or as a natural extension of existing technologies, *technology-pushed* new products are a reality. As opposed to *market-pulled* products, they may take longer to get accepted and the market's reaction may be much slower, but nevertheless, acceptance of some of these products indicates emerging new markets.

Firm's Own Efforts in Breakthrough Developments

Earlier it has been advocated that every firm should develop a futuristic portfolio. Some products in such a portfolio may turn out to be critical breakthroughs and, as such, they can make new markets to emerge.

As Figure 11.3 illustrates, the five key forces end up leading to the development of numerous new products that will be found in emerging niche markets. These emerging niche markets, as they become a reality, will need more varieties of the same products as well as many new products. Here a performance analysis of some of the products our company is particularly interested in may lead the company to establish which newly emerging markets would be more important to enter.

OPPORTUNITY BUDGETING ONCE AGAIN

Although in Chapter 4 a discussion of opportunity budgeting is presented, it is important to reintroduce this concept in our discussion here. If we are questioning our traditionalist point of view and becoming more futuristic, we will analyze emerging new markets and new products within these new markets. As is discussed earlier, based on the projected market opportunities, an *opportunity budget* would allocate the necessary resources to utilize the emerging and projected opportunities to our advantage. The changes in the market due to multitudinous factors cannot be interpreted if the company functions on the basis of its strong traditions alone. Instead, the proactive management would look at changes in the market as opportunities, and by prioritizing these opportunities would develop an opportunity budget so that the changes in the market would become gainful opportunities for the firm. Thus, the proactive management must have a counterchaos human resource development program that can perform well in chaotic market conditions. Developing a learning organization (Chapter 6), and improvisation (Chapter 7), along with cultivating counterchaos markets (Chapter 5), provide the basis to develop and use an opportunity budget and implement it forcefully. Management with such a proactive orientation is constantly in need of new capabilities.

CREATING NEW CAPABILITIES AS THEY APPEAR TO BE NEEDED

All firms have core competencies. By recognizing its core competencies carefully, the firm can clearly define its boundaries as to how far it could go as new opportunities are discovered. Those activities that are performed better than competitors and are critical for the firm's end products or services are core competencies. Only a few firms can make the claim that they know the real strengths that are their core competencies. Defining the core competencies incorrectly can cause serious problems. Here the means and ends must be distinguished. Certain characteristics of the firm such

Figure 11.4.
Budgeting.

	Budgeting Orientation	
	Traditional	Opportunity
Current	Tradition-bound, highly incumbent, very vulnerable	Difficult to implement the opportunity budget, current core competencies are inadequate (vulnerable)
Core Competencies		
	Although there is no opportunity budgeting, the firm understands the need for new core competencies (vulnerable)	The firm understands the need for new core competencies and budgets its resources accordingly (most likely to succeed)
Needed		

as "having quality products" or "having a very good reputation" are ends. They are not core competencies; they are the results of core competencies.[11] The relationship between core competencies and opportunity budgeting is displayed in Figure 11.4.

The upper left quadrant of the exhibit illustrates the worst-case scenario. Traditional orientation in budgeting, coupled with emphasis on current core competencies, makes a firm tradition-bound and suffers from an acute case of incumbency. These conditions make the firm very vulnerable to unexpected and harsh market shocks.

The lower right quadrant of the matrix is the total opposite of the first quadrant. Here the firm is not only using an opportunity budgeting approach but is also acquiring the needed core competencies. Understanding the need for new core competencies and allocating budgetary resources toward their development is the most proactive approach. This situation illustrates the greatest likelihood for survival and success.

Between these two extremes, the firm may have an opportunity budget but not be exploring new emerging opportunities (upper right quadrant), or it may be aware of the needed new core competencies but not willing to allocate budgetary resources (lower left quadrant). In both of these cases, the firm is rather vulnerable to emerging adverse market conditions.

COUNTERCHAOS HUMAN RESOURCE DEVELOPMENT

All organizations have certain core skills that make them able to develop products and services with which they are identified and by which they generate their revenue and profit streams. These core skills are the critical capabilities that create the companies' competitive advantage. In a sense, core skills are collective capabilities of individual firms to implement their strategic visions. Honda has been successful in the United States by having an innovative, simple, low-cost, and quality product appealing to a new breed of customers through a new and noticeably distinctive distribution system.[12] Similarly, Dell has been doing the same things in the personal computer segment of the market. But, as has been stated a few times throughout our discussions, core competencies, based on core skills, are not likely to remain the same. As indicated in Figure 11.4, proactive firms develop their core competencies as the market conditions dictate. Developing such competencies swiftly is the essence of counterchaos human resource development. This way the firm will be in a position to take advantage of unexpected market changes.

CREATING NEW CAPABILITIES FURTHER

The firm's sensitivity to and understanding of its core competencies that enable it to establish its market power and react to market shocks is the essence of its survival and profitability. A proactive corporate entity understands how to dissect a market development and what changes it should make in its core competency areas. Figure 11.5 depicts the details of such process. From changing or unexpected market influences to identifying and, if needed, acquiring new core skills, there is a long and extremely critical way. The firm must act not only effectively but also extremely swiftly. "Effectively" here means the events or adjustments must be interpreted into core competencies and then into core skills that make core competencies a reality. Regardless of the level of effectiveness, if the whole process does not take place swiftly, then the firm is out of luck. This author firmly believes in the statement that "you don't get a second chance to make a first impression." A proactive and counterchaotic firm is already prepared for such situations by having the proper corporate culture, the drive to innovate, futuristic product portfolios, and much improvisational experiences. Here, as seen in Figure 11.5, all of these features become important in terms of acquiring new capabilities.

New Capabilities from Within

Depending upon the extent and the nature of the new core skills, decisions must be made very quickly as to whether the corporate human resources can handle the new situation by employing its existing resources.

Figure 11.5.
Considering New Opportunities and
Reexamining Core Competencies.

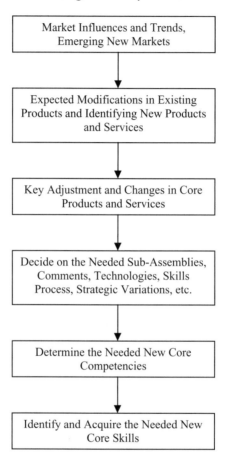

What would it take to acquire or to actualize new skills? Again, here *lean thinking* will not go very far. The decisions must be based on objectivity and sound thinking.

New Capabilities from Without

Once again, the proactive firm must already have some key sources identified in case additional core skills are required. The firm, instead of thinking about downsizing and cost cutting, has to think proactively to assess how these core skills can be acquired. This type of orientation must penetrate throughout the organizational layers so that existing workers understand the changing needs and are not intimidated by the possibility of certain people joining their ranks. The management, needless to say, must be confident of its decision-making process and in its ability to choose the right people for the newly required core skills.

THINKING OUT OF THE BOX

Although throughout this book our discussions imply the need for non-conventional thinking, at this point this concept really comes to life. Let us face it, there are not too many companies, if any at all, thinking ahead for additional core skills and how they can be acquired. This is thinking out of the box in its most effective way. Without such vision, orientation, and dedication, the counterchaos spirit cannot be constructed. This orientation is NOT the "we have been doing this way traditionally" orientation. Every manager, every CEO, every managerial aspirant must understand the critical importance of thinking out of the box and indeed must be engaged in it extensively. Once again, they must be able to distinguish between wishful thinking and strategy.

CONVERGENCE AND DIVERGENCE DICHOTOMY

During the past three decades or so, diversification in the economy has been facilitated by unfriendly takeovers, mergers, and acquisitions. Diversification often is perceived to be the convergence of two or three industries. If a pharmaceutical company merges with a company that is a distribution specialist, or when a gasoline-accelerated automobile is merged with an electric-powered car in terms of generating a hybrid, convergence of multiple industries takes place to create new products, which, in fact, may be new industries. Convergence, by definition, leads in the direction of dramatically new products and, indeed, even in the emergence of disruptive technologies.

However, computers are not the result of the convergence of calculators and electricity. Nor is the fuel-cell-driven automobile the convergence of two industries. Thus, some developments are the result of divergence, and others are the result of convergence. Regardless, one must realize that divergence is a complete deviation from the conventional way of thinking, whereas convergence is conventional thinking finding a way to bridge itself to other conventional thinking, even though the outcome is not quite conventional.

Divergence, however, is strictly thinking out of the box. It represents a totally new way of thinking and, perhaps, doing. As a company, it may be critical to follow possible convergences and potential divergences as future chaos-creating forces. Although both processes are powerful, it is maintained here that divergence may create more shocking results. For instance, divergence may indicate that instead of a more powerful airplane, missile technology may become the pivotal force in transportation. In such a situation, the results would be more shocking, since a missile can take passengers from the United States to Australia in a matter of minutes. More on convergence and divergence thinking is presented in Chapter 13.

WHAT GOES UP DOES NOT HAVE TO COME DOWN

Regardless of the convergence or divergence dichotomy, it is critical that a major new development not be taken as flimsy and faddish. At first, department stores considered discount stores to be whimsical and short-lived. Clearly, any development and/or breakthrough is likely to be powerful enough to make an impact and last a long time. Once again, divergence and convergence would lead in the direction of nontraditional development. Thus, if we are not tied down to some powerful traditional orientation, we will find out the powerful impact of dramatically new developments, and we will learn both to survive and benefit from them.

CRITICAL COUNTERCHAOS CHECKLIST

1. Are we cognizant of the existence of inertia traps?
2. Do we understand that internal paths of least resistance are traditions that tie down our progress?
3. What happens to traditions as we are challenged by emerging disruptive technologies?
4. Can we tell what questionable traditions we suffer from and how we can eliminate them?
5. What do we learn from the lean thinking credo that is applicable to all of our activities?

SUMMARY

All firms can easily fall into an inertia trap. The firm's strategic frames, resources, processes that it uses, its relationships and values should always be questioned.

Traditional thinking is likely to be dysfunctional in a very dynamic market. When we are facing chaos, we cannot be traditional and forced to not make any changes or adjustments. The corporate culture that provides vision and values that are different than traditional ways is the prerequisite. Corporate culture can move the company from conventional ways of thinking to proactive ways of thinking. The company cannot remain an inactive incumbent in a dynamic market. Hence we must watch for and examine newly emerging new markets. Here, the firm must utilize an opportunity budget to generate a newly needed core competency to survive chaotic conditions. Developing new core competencies is related to obtaining the necessary new skills. Convergence and divergence are considered as the forces behind most powerful market shocks. And it is posited that the market shocks that are generated by these two power sources are likely to live a long time.

Chapter 12

It Is Not What They Do—It Is What We Should Be Doing

Although Trout (2004) maintains that to be successful companies must be competition-oriented, they must identify the weaknesses of competitors and attack them, this author believes that being proactive goes beyond that. If the company has the drive to innovate and the imagination to support such a drive, it will innovate for the future rather than innovating to improve the past. In other words, it will go to where the puck is likely to be. If we are a company dealing with high-tech products, instead of making incremental changes on existing high-tech products, we may have to research on nanotechnologies and make sure that we are the trendsetter.

WE MUST IMAGINE A DESIRED FUTURE

Most companies use business forecasting, whereas strategic foresight is preferable. While forecasting deals with logical reasoning, and quantitative analysis predicts the future, foresight employs trend information and knowledge of market developments to cultivate imaginative thinking to foresee likely emerging opportunities or chaotic happenings.[1] Since there is not enough sensitivity about the relationship between market conditions and strategic choices, it is difficult to manage the desired future. However, creating the desired future and, hence, overcoming market adversities, if and when they occur, depends on comprehending and working with the interaction between market conditions and strategy. This is how a strategic supremacy is established. Crate and Barrel or Williams-Sonoma, among hundreds of others, managed to achieve such strategic supremacy.

ESTABLISHING STRATEGIC SUPREMACY

If our firm has the capability to establish or change the rules of the game in the marketplace anytime it needs to and thus control or ride evolutions (or preferably revolutions), then it has strategic supremacy. Industries and markets are not stationary. Rapidly globalizing knowledge-intensive industries and resultant changes in competition and markets necessitate employing disruptive behavior on the part of the firm that is creating strategic supremacy by deviating from traditions, changing the rules of winning and, above all, by providing radically new type of value to customers.[2] When Starbucks started offering exotic coffees in attractive surroundings in the form of affordable luxury, the company invented the future of the coffee industry by redefining the rules and disrupting the market conditions.[3] Similarly, when Gillette introduced the Mach 3 razor, it was attempting to redefine the rules of competition and thereby disrupting the market conditions.

In D'Aveni's words:[4]

Too little attention has been paid to the differences between the strategies of dominant incumbents (maintaining the current environment) and the strategies of challengers (disrupting the current environment). Studies of what I call hyper-competition have provided important insights into the inextricably intertwined relationships among disruption, patterns of turbulence, the rules of competition, and the definition of the playing field.

Not only should the firm be primed to understand the nature of current competition and the characteristics of its current markets, but it must also be in a position to evaluate the appropriate strategic paradigm in its industry. This means the firm is capable of assessing the current rules of the game however changeable they may be. Here the proactive firm attempting to achieve *strategic supremacy* may be able to redefine the rules in the industry by carefully calculated *disruptions*. It is maintained here that by such efforts to achieve strategic supremacy, as long as the efforts are proactive and in the right direction, the firm can be less vulnerable to chaotic market influences. Here it is advocated that the old cliché "best defense is offense" is a reasonable proposition if implemented and used properly. In addition to the proper corporate culture, fostering the drive to innovate must be fed with imagination and boldness to set trends.

HOW CAN WE BECOME A TRENDSETTER?

Although many firms opt for the path of least resistance by erecting entry barriers, reducing buyer or supplier powers, striking oligopolistic bargains, or eliminating substitutes by mergers and acquisitions, these are not necessarily workable in the face of radical changes in the market along with disruptive technologies and other powerful market developments. Such passive orientation and attempting to maintain or even enhance the *status quo* can be devastating.

Here, perhaps the only workable choice is establishing the rules of competition. Those who can become trendsetters can generate and enhance wealth in the economy. General Motors, for example, spent millions of dollars over a number of decades to build a barrier to entry to the auto industry by supporting thousands of service dealers. But then the Japanese designed cars that did not need service, entered the American market, and captured some 30 percent of it.[5]

Trendsetting, therefore, is related to successfully redefining the rules of the game. This can be achieved in many ways, among which are engaging in price wars, advertising wars, R&D wars, and above all, competitive strategies that are utilized by companies to generate competitive advantage.

Although throughout this book we have been discussing ways to protect the firm from and take advantage of chaotic market influences, it is critical to realize that hypercompetitive environments created by these influences are also very lucrative if the firm can successfully participate in them.

In earlier years, conventional wisdom advocated that the lack of rivalry in stable markets is attractive. But recent analyses indicate that hypercompetitive environments, because of increased competition, are better to participate in if an industry is truly focused on new and different basis of rivalries to enhance consumer values. Just what are our aspirations here becomes a critical question.

Our Aspirations Must Be Declared with a Sense of Urgency

Aspiring to become a trendsetter and becoming one are not the same. If we are aspiring to become a trendsetter because we believe we can change or modify the rules of competition and establish competitive advantage, then this aspiration must be taken very seriously. As was discussed earlier, agility with a strong sense of urgency is necessary if we want to isolate ourselves from chaotic market developments. It must be reiterated that a firm does not have to be the most powerful or number one firm to be a trendsetter. Here it is posited that those firms that are cognizant of the importance of interaction between their strategies and the competitive environment and use this interaction to their advantage have a good chance of becoming trendsetters.

Proactivity Is Achieving the Desired Future

Attempting to become a trendsetter and hence protecting oneself against unexpected market adversities by modifying or changing the rules of competition is proactivity. However, the firm must have what it takes. The Cray Computer Corporation, a company that was founded on the premise of the supercomputer, could not continue operations due to lack of funds.[6]

Assuming the fact that the firm may have what it takes, how do we know the desired future? After all, most members of top management may know the business and all of its intimate details, but that is not enough. It is not certain that their planning process, indeed their planning skills, have changed radically in years. Thus, knowing the desired future and planning for it are not givens. Proactivity, or innovative planning, is not and should not be limited to just a few administrators. In fact, Bill Gates has stated that Microsoft's response to the Internet came from a number of dedicated employees. Seeking out new ideas and democratizing the strategy process are essential prerequisites for proactivity.

We Work for the Best

Turock[7] maintains that strategy is work in progress. Hence, it needs attention every day, not just a week during the annual strategy retreat. Obviously, when a firm deviates from conventional wisdom or the incumbent status, there are possibilities not only to succeed a bit but also to lose big. Certainly, the firm is trying to achieve the best and not the worst. Effective proactivity is the only way we may expect the best to happen as we become a trendsetter and take charge. Here the firm is managing probabilities. Probability for success and resultant avoidance of chaotic market influences are related to our discussion throughout this book. Here we must talk more about creativity as it relates to proactivity.

WE MUST FOSTER CREATIVITY

The ability to establish or change the rules of the game and, as a result, to initiate revolution or at least be an early participant in it means strategic supremacy. Such supremacy cannot exist without powerful creativity. The firm must be in a position to think the unthinkable and try the impossible through creativity and, perhaps, improvisation. Thus, creativity must be unleashed and sustained in our organization.

Target, for instance, attempted successfully to generate new luxury products for its large middle-class markets. In order to accomplish this, the company relied on the help of world-renowned designers such as Michael Graves, Philip Starck, and Cynthia Rowley, among others, to develop high-end designer housewares.[8]

UNLEASHING CREATIVITY

In every organization, and in every company, there is bundled-up creativity that needs to be unleashed. Figure 12.1 illustrates criteria to unleash this essential ingredient of proactivity. The exhibit dwells upon eight powerful stimulants of creativity.

Starting with Freedom

Freedom in an organization is having alternatives and choosing one. This is certainly based on freedom of thinking. Democratization of strategic planning and decision-making in proactive companies is the basis for creativity. Instead of managing subordinates, working with coworkers is the essence of a creative atmosphere stimulated by freedom.

Realizing Uncertainty

Throughout a firm, the realization that there is uncertainty in our industry, market, and industrial environment opens the door to creativity. Uncertainty and its realization facilitate thinking out of the box for solutions. If there are serious uncertainties about the firm, its actions, and its opportunities, it becomes necessary to think about likely and unlikely alternative solutions.

Cognizance of Changes

Ability to detect changes at the earliest possible stage is not an automatic activity. Our discussion throughout the book has hinted about the importance of understanding and managing external changes generated by unexpected chaotic developments. This is a special feature that proactive managements must always try to acquire. But changes lead to uncertainty, and managing uncertainty is unleashing creativity.

Figure 12.1.
Unleashing Creativity.

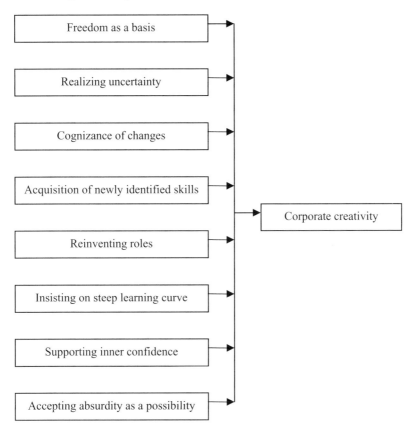

Acquisition of Newly Identified Skills

Partially because of the realization of uncertainty, and the cognizance of change, acquisition of newly identified skills, by definition, expands the capability spectrum of the firm. Many unplanned but positive skills may show up unexpectedly and further stimulate the firm's overall creativity.

Reinventing Roles

If the company moves away from superior-subordinate relationships to a more democratized format, then many jobs need to be redefined. Because of organizational restructuring and because of redescribed and newly identified roles, creativity is further stimulated.

Insisting on a Steep Learning Curve

In Chapter 5, we discussed the importance of a learning organization in facing accelerating market adversities. A truly proactive firm would make it a corporate responsibility for everyone in it to learn as much as possible and would facilitate this learning process *not as an expense but as a major investment*. Here, learning more is always better.

Supporting Inner Confidence

Being part of the organization and playing a role in its future is not only gratifying but also a reinforcement to self-confidence and self-worth. Developing a corporate culture that aligns employee functions and behaviors with the organization's futuristic orientation, by definition, stimulates overall creativity.

Accepting Absurdity as a Possibility

In a traditional "this is the how we do things around here" orientation, there is usually a tendency to trivialize ideas and new ways of thinking and looking at different alternatives. If the company wants to stimulate creativity, it must pay attention to all ideas. No idea is totally absurd, and no idea should be dismissed upfront.

As we unleash creativity in our organization, we stimulate imagination in our company. Without an imagination and a sense of belongingness on the part of its people, it is questionable just how a firm can survive in extremely dynamic and unfriendly markets.

NOT MANAGING PEOPLE BUT WORKING WITH PEOPLE

Drucker[9] stated, "one does not 'manage' people. The task is to lead people. And the goal is to make productive the specific strengths and knowledge of each individual." In other words, instead of managing people, we will be able to manage the work well if we work with people. Collins[10] argues that freedom and responsibility within a given framework implies the presence of a culture with *discipline* that gives enough freedom to cohorts so that the system rather than the people can be managed well.

In Figure 12.1, it is implied that as the creativity in the corporate entity is unleashed, developing a "creativity space" for each and every person is set aside. Such a creativity space would provide an opportunity to become more professional, more proactive, and more of an asset than a liability.

Thus, this whole process is an extremely important investment in the company's future. Such a forward-looking idea as a creativity space needs to be developed according to prevailing conditions, resources, and perceived needs. It will have to be tailored for every special, individual situation.[11]

BALANCING INTERNAL AND EXTERNAL COMMUNICATION

The company's connectedness to the industry and to markets, that is, part of its external communication (the other part of external communication is the firm's promotional efforts) must be not only intact but also must be interpreted carefully and swiftly.

Enthusiasm Begets Enthusiasm

If and when external communication reveals new and unexpected aberrations in the market, and if these are interpreted enthusiastically and shared with the people in the organization, such enthusiasm would generate equally important enthusiasm among all ranks.

Strategic Innovation Must Flourish

The level of enthusiasm, this author believes, has much to do with strategic innovation. Understanding the corporate plans for counterchaos strategies and relating these plans to individuals' mindsets cannot help but be instrumental in the flourishing of strategic innovation. But, it must also be considered that if the conditions in the market are changing drastically and the strategic innovation is not flourishing adequately, the firm can be in a dramatically dangerous position.

Talent Must Be Revered

In the face of accelerating market adversities, talent in our company must be revered. It is this talent that will find modifications of the existing strategies or will propose dramatic new *game plans* that may be needed.

Autonomy Must Be Encouraged

In order to generate dramatic new game plans, not only must talent be revered, but also individuals would be given enough autonomy for independent thinking and idea generation. Autonomy here would indicate the opportunity of thinking out of the box.

Creative Human Capital Is Priceless

It is rather clear that effective proactivity is intimately connected to creative human capital. In the 1980s and 1990s, there was a movement named "down-sizing," which has subsequently been renamed "right-sizing." However, this author has expressed his perception of the incorrectness of this concept as *wrong-sizing*. It is clear by now that without creative human capital, the corporate entity cannot go far; in fact, in an extremely dynamic market, it is doomed. Thus the corporate human capital, if it is creative enough, is *priceless*. It will be a terrible mistake to think of it as a total cost factor. On the contrary, the human capital must be evaluated and developed not on the basis of cost but also on the basis of talent and opportunity.

SELF-EVALUATION AT THE CORPORATE LEVEL

Self-awareness of the corporate entity comes into focus here. This is creating a balance between external market conditions and functions of the corporate entity. The balancing factor here can be called the game plan or the overall corporate strategy. All companies, whether they are cognizant of it or not, have a strategic posture.

What Is Our Strategic Posture?

Who are we? What are we trying to do? And how are we doing it? These are the critical questions regarding the firm's strategic posture. If the firm has a strategic posture that is clearly defined and followed, the chances of not being stunned by unexpected and accelerating market adversities are good. Thus, the firm should know the general parameters of its strategic options. There are certain generic strategy alternatives.

GENERIC STRATEGY POSTURES

Table 12.1 describes clearly the nine generic strategies and illustrates each by giving examples. It must be reiterated that the generic characteristics of these strategies imply that they are applicable to any situation where one party may wish to gain a competitive edge. This is not only true in marketing but perhaps in all other competitive activities, such as sports or card games.

One last point about Table 12.1 is that it does not purport to be totally exhaustive. The author's research has revealed only these nine; however, it is quite likely that there are others. Perhaps one of the key contributions of this chapter is to stimulate thinking and research in such a way that more generic strategies may be discovered.

The following is a brief description of the nine generic strategies:

- *Leader:* the leader is often the largest and the most established company in the market. IBM is the leader in computers. Hewlett-Packard spends over $5 billion on R&D to remain the leader in high-tech industries.
- *Challenger:* This is the up-and-coming company, which is perhaps the most dynamic firm in the industry. Apple was a challenger in the computer market. Today, perhaps, Dell has taken that position.
- *Follower:* This is an imitating firm, which follows the leader's footsteps. IBM has many clones. Many small companies produce IBM-type products at a slightly lower price. Dell does not try to improve computers and computer-related products. It simply sells the product at a slightly lower price and distributes the merchandise more efficiently.
- *Nicher:* There are always dynamic small companies who can do well in a well-defined corner of the market. Nichers choose the market segment carefully and establish themselves well. Zenith has been trying to corner the government and education niches for its computers.[12]
- *Explorer:* Some companies believe that developing new products and new markets is the key for survival. Explorers put heavy emphasis on R&D and mergers and acquisition. They differentiate their products, markets, and strategic postures by exploring. 3M is well known for putting special emphasis on innovation and development of new products. Casio constantly moves into new markets with new products.
- *Defender:* Some companies are situated well in the market and take a reactive posture. They try to maintain their market position by taking advantage of their current status and perhaps by harvesting past investments. For example, Sears is trying to defend its number one retailer position by refocusing on retailing. Sears' announced plans are to harvest some of its financial subsidiaries and concentrate on offering multiple brands at attractive prices.
- *Mixer:* It is not necessary that a company will choose only one of the above six strategies. Some large and diversified companies may use different strategies for different aspects of their business. They deliberately mix their strategies. Procter and Gamble uses different strategies for its different product groups. Johnson & Johnson is using different strategies for each of its three key areas: household items, pharmaceuticals, and medical equipment.

Table 12.1
Generic Strategy Alternatives

Strategy	Key Features	Game Plan Emphasis	Advantages	Typical Examples
Leader	Often, the first and the most established company in the market	To keep ahead by heavy promotion and research	Survival and prosperity through growth and reputation	IBM, Xerox, etc. who have set the tone of new industries
Challenger	The most dynamic company in the market	Challenge the leader through innovativeness, research and development, and aggressive marketing	Survival and prosperity through accelerated growth and increased reputation	Apple has been challenging IBM particularly in the PC area
Follower	Strictly a "me too" company. Follows the leader's footsteps; imitates perhaps at a slightly lower price	Choose the right leader and follow its activities and imitate. Use reduced price or slightly varied marketing activity for similar products that the leader has	Taking advantage of the leader's accomplishments, prospering through the growth that the leader developed in the market, and minimized risk	All the clones of IBM follow IBM's new models and imitate them
Nicher	A dynamic small company that can do some things well	Choose the market segment, establish itself there well, and continue being effective in that niche.	Survival and prosperity through good performance in a well-defined market by avoiding major competition	Jeep for years used the niche that demanded a sturdy four-wheel drive vehicle
Explorer	Always looking for new products or new markets. A company with vision and a sense of timeliness	Heavy emphasis on R&D as well as on mergers and acquisition	Survival and prosperity through diversification	Casio is always looking for new hi-tech products for various markets

Defender	Company tries to maintain its market position and protects its specific niches (if any)	Special emphasis on reactive orientation based on market audits. Taking advantage of the firm's current status and harvesting	Continued prosperity by maintaining the firm's relative position	Hertz, A&P, or even GM are (or were) No. 1 and trying to maintain (or regain) this position
Mixer	Company tries to maintain or improve its market position by using more than one of the above six strategies	Special emphasis on versatility and varied nature of the markets that company is engaged in	Continued prosperity by maintaining or improving the firm's position in different markets	Many highly diversified companies such as Dow Chemical or DuPont have different strategies for major product lines
Scrambler	Company tries to maintain or improve its market position by changing industry or markets while ahead and trying to avoid competition or showdowns.	Special emphasis on market intelligence, flexibility, and versatility in moving in and out of markets	Continued prosperity by growth situation in different industries and markets	3M has been involved in perpetual market creation by continual reinvention
Guerilla Fighter	Company tries to maintain its existence any way it can.	Emphasizing uniqueness of a very small business by establishing very close personal relationships.	Establishing some monopolistic competition power.	A boutique in an inner city.

- *Scrambler:* There are some companies that try to improve their market position by changing industry or markets. Thus, they avoid competition or showdowns. They take advantage of growth markets. They blur the picture by scrambling, making it difficult for competitors to compete.
- *Guerrilla Fighter:* There are many very small companies that are in a struggle for survival. They will do whatever is needed to survive and perhaps eventually to prosper. Entrepreneurships and small businesses are in this category. Their key strength is personalizing their relationship with their customers and providing special services. A boutique in the inner city behaves in the described manner.

The next major consideration is to determine which of these, and perhaps other, generic strategies is the most suitable for a firm, given its internal and external parameters. Parameters here imply the conditions over which the firm has little or no control. It is maintained here that these parameters determine the suitability of the generic strategy. Thus, it is posited in this article that the generic strategy selection is not *situation-specific.* It is, rather, *parameter-specific.* Although some authors advocate that the marketing strategy choice process is primarily dependent upon understanding and evaluating strategic situation, a different orientation is taken here. Situation specificity implies that strategy will change as the market conditions change. Thus the changing conditions in the market in the short run will determine the firm's strategic option. The situational changes would perhaps modify the implementation of the generic strategy but would not influence the strategic choice itself. On the other hand, the proposed parameters will enable the marketer to identify the generic strategy that is most suitable for the business in question. Hence, the generic strategy choice is parameter-specific. In Table 12.2, six specific parameters are identified.

PARAMETERS LEADING TO GENERIC STRATEGY SELECTION

Although there may be others and, specifically, there may be special ones based on the unique characteristics of the industry, the firm, or the market, the six parameters depicted in Table 12.2 are considered to be most critical in choosing the generic strategy.

Market Characteristics

Depending upon whether the market is growing, stabilized, or declining, the strategy selection varies significantly. Being the leader, for instance, or the challenger in a declining market is hardly an appropriate approach.

Table 12.2
Parameters Leading to Strategy Selection

Strategic Options	Market Conditions	Competition	Company Size	Stage in Company Life Cycle	Company Marketing Philosophy	Company Support Strengths
Leader	Growth or stabilized markets	Not keen present competition but high potential competition	Large company with ample resources	Growth or mature company	Firm commitment to marketing concept in a systems setting	All around support resources
Challenger	Growth markets	Present competition is becoming keen, future competition is likely to level off	Large company with ample resources	Growth or mature company	Firm commitment to marketing concept with some emphasis on special product or product line	Strong R&D capabilities
Follower	Stabilized or declining markets	Competition leveled off and is likely to stay that way	Medium- to small-size company with modest resources	Growth or mature companies	Firm commitment to selling concept based on the Leader's marketing orientation	Strong sales and promotional skills and resources
Nicher	Stabilized or even declining markets	Stabilized competition; no room for new competitors	Medium- to small-size	Introductory or growth company	Firm commitment to marketing concept in a systems setting	All around support resources (scaled down)
Explorer	Growing new markets	Little competition at present high potential competition	Large company with ample resources	Introductory, growth, or mature company	Emphasis on selling concept, some commitment to product concept	Special resources in promotion and R&D

(continued)

Table 12.2
(*continued*)

Strategic Options	Market Conditions	Competition	Company Size	Stage in Company Life Cycle	Company Marketing Philosophy	Company Support Strengths
Defender	Stabilized or declining markets	Leveled off competition with possible modest new competition	Large or medium size	Mature or decline company	Firm commitment to marketing concept	All around support resources (scaled down)
Mixer	Growth stabilized and decline markets	Various levels of competition in different markets	Large company with ample resources	Mature or decline company	Firm commitment to a total systems concept	All around support resources
Scrambler	Growth or stabilized markets	Many new competitors competing at different levels	Large company with ample resources	Mature company	Heavy emphasis on market intelligence systems leading to a firm commitment to total systems concept	Very strong market intelligence system and adequate resources to switch markets and industries
Guerilla Fighter	A very small portion of a growth or stabilized markets	Much competition and most are using similar strategy.	Very small company with limited resources.	Probably in-troductory stage	Heavy emphasis on service and customer satisfaction	Very limited but unique products and personal service

However, being a defender or a mixer is quite appropriate for this kind of market condition.

Competition

Competition changes constantly in terms of its intensity and nature. If competition is getting keener, being a scrambler is clearly better than being a follower. While a follower will have to face increasing competition, a scrambler successfully avoids it. Competition may get keener and may also change its nature. New competition coming from new companies that are mixers or explorers may change the nature of competition in that market. In such cases, being a scrambler or a challenger may be necessary.

Company Size

The size of a company and related resources and capabilities establish a clear-cut parameter as to which one of the eight strategies can be chosen. When it is time to develop an overall marketing strategy, it must be understood that the size is a given and is not likely to change unless the company is pursuing a challenger strategy by growth and acquisitions. While, for instance, a company needs to be large to be a leader, a small company is likely to be a nicher. Similarly, the firm has to be large enough in order to be an explorer or a scrambler. However, it certainly is likely to be smaller than the leader. Without appropriate size and resources, it is almost impossible for the firm to assume a leadership role. Finally, very small firms have hardly any other strategy option other than guerilla fighter.

Stage in Company Life Cycle

The stage of the company life cycle, by definition, establishes a key parameter in choosing a generic strategy or not choosing many others. A well-established firm that has assumed a leadership position in the market, such as IBM, cannot suddenly change its strategy to something like niching or defending. If the company has reached a clearly identifiable stage in its life cycle, it cannot suddenly change its strategic posture, particularly if the company has achieved that particular stage with a clear-cut strategic option. In other words, if the firm has been an explorer for all of its life, it will be almost impossible for it to become a leader or a scrambler during its maturity or decline stages. In other words, it is harder to change the strategy as the firm matures. Indeed this is why very old and well-established firms find themselves in trouble as they experience decline. This is one of the reasons why Singer in sewing machines and A&P in groceries have found themselves in trouble. Both companies have been the leader in their respective industries for many decades.

Company Marketing Philosophy

Marketing has evolved on the basis of a series of eras. One classification is: production, sales, marketing management, environmental, and total systems. These five eras, although they have evolved in time, are still substantially coexisting. Thus, companies, in their efforts to develop strategies, may be emphasizing one at the expense of others. Although no corporation can solely emphasize only one, it is possible to favor one while not totally ignoring others. As depicted in Table 12.2, the leader may have a firm commitment to implementing the marketing concept. The leader may accomplish this by using a systems approach and penetrating all the components of the company with the same philosophy and practice.

The challenger, on the other hand, will have to put a special emphasis on its competitive edge. This edge may be exercised by a unique product or product line. The follower may be imitating the leader and perhaps may be attempting to sell more forcefully than the leader. The nicher is, in a sense, the leader in a specific segment of the market. Hence, it may be doing what a leader would do, only at a smaller scale.

The explorer is basically putting emphasis on selling and perhaps on production. The explorer may be looking for new avenues and new horizons. In its pursuits to find new and better opportunities, the explorer may be creating new products and then trying to sell them rigorously. In a sense, Xerox started that way. Casio may be coined an explorer, pursuing similar strategic paths in multiple product and multiple industry areas.[13]

A defender may be considered a leader who has gone past the maturity stage in its life cycle. From that perspective, it is almost by definition that a defender, just like a leader, would be committed to the marketing concept. The company has reached its leadership position that way and is accustomed to implementing marketing concept as a defender also.

The mixer, perhaps more than others, looks at itself as a total system and tries to balance between its internal and external well-being. Thus it uses any and all of the generic strategies as the system deems necessary.

The scrambler is an avoider. As such, its dependence on market intelligence systems feeds into a firm dependence on the total system's orientation for survival and growth.

Finally, the guerilla fighter is a street brawler. It will do whatever is necessary to survive. It does not have elaborate strategic plans, but it reads swiftly and develops critical personal relationships with its customers.

Company Support Strengths

In order to choose the most appropriate generic strategy and to implement it successfully, the firm needs to have certain resources, which are coined "company support strengths." Table 12.2 describes the most necessary company support strengths. For instance, a company cannot be a leader without appropriate support resources. The company must have the ability to out-sell, out-promote, out-price, and out-produce everyone in the industry, among other functional activities.

Similarly, a company cannot be a challenger without strong R&D capabilities that will give it a competitive edge in terms of developing a better and more efficient product line. In recent years, IBM is being challenged by Apple on this type of activity. Apple has developed enough uniqueness, particularly in desktop printing, which is giving IBM strong competition.

The follower has to have effective sales and promotional skills and support resources. The follower is basically imitating the leader. If the following company has the same type of products as the leader, with strong sales and promotional strengths, the company can easily make inroads into the leader's market. Amdahl Computers has done exactly that to compete with IBM in IBM's market.

The nicher has to have an all-around support system because it is a leader in that particular niche. The defender and mixer type of strategy also call for all-around support services. If Ricoh were to be able to compete with Xerox in the copying industry, it is likely to follow a nicher or scrambler strategy. In both cases it has to have a unique service support system for satisfying its customers' needs.

The scrambler must have a very strong market intelligence system. This intelligence system has to be supported with, again, all-around support resources so that it can switch markets and industries.

Finally, the guerrilla fighter must have some unique products or services or a combination that will appeal to its very limited market, such as in the case of a very small ethnic restaurant.

WHO ARE WE? CAN WE SWITCH? HOW? WHY?

It is clear that the generic strategies presented in the earlier section are not constants but identify where the company has been and where it is headed. The assessment of the strategic posture in the face of market developments is very critical. Assessment of this type, and accordingly deciding what (if any) modifications need to be made, is the livelihood of the corporate entity. The firm has to be on top of its strategic posture and its success. It must be iterated that the strategic posture mostly to manage the present and try to remain powerful for managing the future can go in the direction of being market driven or being a market driver. The driver is more futuristic whereas the driven is trying to manage the present.

CRITICAL COUNTERCHAOS CHECKLIST

1. Can we imagine a desired future for our company that is realistic?
2. Are we powerful enough to change the rules of competition by achieving strategic supremacy?
3. How can we become a trendsetter by successfully redefining the rules of the game?
4. Can we foster creativity so that proactively we achieve the desired future?
5. What are our bundled-up creativity features that need to be unleashed and how do we manage them in balancing the present and the future?

SUMMARY

This chapter is about what we should be doing. If we don't know we cannot DO. Turock[14] cites a very important quote: "Uncertainty reveals genius; security conceals it." We must feel only fairly secure about our position and our markets. But we must be able to plan effectively and, if necessary, change decisively.[15]

It is posited that we must imagine a desired future and work for it. This would necessitate becoming a trendsetter. Our aspirations must be articulated in an urgent manner. This type of proactivity can give us the best or the worst; hence, we must work for the best.

Becoming a trendsetter implies fostering creativity. Corporate creativity *must be* unleashed. Here it is clear that creative corporate human capital is priceless.

All in all, we must know what we are doing, where we are headed, and how to get there. This orientation requires an understanding and selection of generic corporate strategies. Nine such strategies are identified in the chapter. Just how we decide which one we should pursue depends on at least six corporate considerations that need to be studied extremely carefully.

Chapter 13

What Are Those Markets Anyway?

We live, function, succeed, prosper, and lose in a marketing system. It is simply not clear if those who pay lip service to the market and indeed to its sanctity really understand it. The simplistic definition that is present in every marketing textbook is that markets are people with the willingness and ability to buy.

MARKETS ARE PEOPLE BUT . . .

Certainly without people there is no market. Thus people are the necessary ingredient, but this is hardly sufficient to understand, to satisfy and, indeed, to prosper on. Just what kind of people, how do they behave, what are their likes and dislikes, how do they communicate, how do they display pleasure and satisfaction? This list of questions could go on almost indefinitely. There are a few basic points that are important. First, markets are not homogeneous; therefore, you cannot say that if you have seen one consumer, you have seen them all. Markets are composed of many components that are referred to as segments. These segments are identifiable, measurable, significant, accessible, and actionable. While significant homogeneity in terms of likes, needs, and behaviors exists within these segments individually, between segments there is much heterogeneity. The greater the heterogeneity among identified market segments, the more effective the segment identification individually. If market segments are identified effectively, then it becomes clear that the ability to buy as well as the willingness to buy vary significantly from one market segment to another.

WILLINGNESS AND ABILITY TO BUY MAKE THE DIFFERENCE

Since markets are not homogeneous and since the firm needs to stand out from its competition and be identified by its markets, it has to segment. In the dramatically hypercompetitive markets of the present times, rivalry has been not only in product and service development and R&D, it has extended into price wars, advertising wars, and logistics wars as well. However, price, advertising, and logistics, despite the fact that they are very important, play a slightly secondary role to overall strategy development and the match between that strategy and the target markets of the firm.

The old saying, "all roads lead to Rome" may not be correct today in the 21st century, but "all attempts and activities towards generating consumer value take place in markets" is very realistic.

The closer and stronger the relation of the firm is to its target markets, the better are the chances for the chaotic influences not to hit the firm uncontrollably. However, target markets, just as everything else in the economy, change. As the changes take place, the firm either manages to stay on top of these changes and modify the rules of competition, or simply adapt to them. If these two options are not workable, the firm redirects its efforts toward other and newly emerging target markets. Regardless of which one of these three approaches is establishing the rules of competition, adapting to changes, or moving into other market segments, the firm needs to stand out from its competition and be identified by its chosen target markets. Thus, the firm must differentiate itself by creating a unique position in the market place, permitting itself to tailor specific products to the needs of market segments that are targeted. This is true for Dell computers, Lamborghini cars, Ricoh copiers, Bayer, Aspirin, or the like.[1]

It is maintained that in hypercompetitive modern markets, rivalry is rewarded if the rules of competition (or winning) are exercised by radically new or substantially more powerful types of customer value.[2] Without near perfect knowledge of the market and near perfect communication with it, such an accomplishment is not possible.

THE MARKET AS A COMMUNICATION NETWORK

Although it is not within the constraints of this book, communication or advertising and other promotional activities must be considered from proactive and counterchaos perspectives. Indeed, markets are people with willingness and ability to buy. However, influencing these people with our products or services is strictly our responsibility.

In modern and hypercompetitive markets, there are many sellers, many offerings, many buyers, and a very complex communication network among these parties. Thus it is not only understanding the needs and competition in the market place, but also particularly being successfully involved in the communication network, which will enable a firm to establish market supremacy. Without communication, consumers or buyers do not know that the products and services needed exist. Similarly, without communication the suppliers of the products and services will not be able to inform prospective buyers. Thus, the presence of the market can be associated with the extensiveness of the ongoing communications network.

WHERE ARE CONSUMERS HEADED?

If the firm wants to go where the puck is likely to be, it will be important to assess just what is happening to consumers. Niche markets are emerging from left and right. From the followers of South Beach diet to new coffee lovers who frequent Starbucks, or wine lovers who put special emphasis on Kendall-Jackson wines.

There are numerous emerging consumer trends that are generating new opportunities for new class luxury products and services.[3] Among these trends are: people are marrying later, are having fewer children, and are more sophisticated. They have a bit more money since they buy their necessities from discounters, and they are getting divorced more often; hence in general people are displaying a need for some special products and services that will make them appear more dynamic with more refined tastes. They buy the new luxury goods and services partially as stress relief and partially just for the love of it. In either case these groups of consumers are looking for goods with very distinct characteristics. Such emerging needs give rise to people such as Ely Callaway who created Callaway Golf, Pleasant Rowland who created The American Girl doll, Fred Carl, Jr., who developed Viking kitchen appliances, and Jim Koch who created Samuel Adams beer. There are hundreds of such inventors who have successfully developed new luxury products. Perhaps the most important common denominator among these people is that they not only thought out of the box, but also actually entered the market out of the box. They all have done different things in their lives rather than working in the areas where they developed new luxury products. In other words, they were not preconditioned to think within the box regarding the new industry and/or the new niche market they entered.

In these emerging niche markets personal influences or what is also called *buzz marketing* becomes extremely critical. In buzz marketing heavy reliance on word-of-mouth advertising pays off. Generating a buzz effect is a critical activity of the modern counterchaos marketer. There may be numerous ways of achieving a buzz effect. However, each time there is an effort to reach out to an emerging niche market, a bottom-up buzz effect needs to be developed for both formation of the niche market as well as the company providing the new luxury product or service line. After all until potential buyers learn about the product or the service from their "coolest" friends or the people from whom they receive opinions or new ideas, a buzz effect cannot be achieved. This is what Chrysler did before introducing the PT Cruiser. The company planted multiple early units in rental fleets in trendy communities to plant the seeds of a buzz effect. Similarly, South Beach Diet, Starbucks, or Kendall-Jackson, among many others, succeed because the buzz information is authentic.[4]

The futuristic orientation of creators of new luxuries is a critical evidence of the decision makers' capability of avoiding chaos that will be inevitable if they do nothing. Where the puck is likely to be there are many fortunes to be made.

CONTROLLING THE MARKET NETWORK IS CONTROLLING THE MARKET

Entering the market successfully implies primarily being in a position to make a major impact in the already existing communications network.

J. Paul Getty, the petroleum tycoon, was known for having said, "If I want to gamble, I buy the casino." In controlling communications, with all due respect to Mr. Getty's position, it does not mean the firm buys the mass media but improves the odds to achieve successful communication. This can be achieved by being in control of its communication process and making a very strong impact on the already existing communication network. Briefly, at least four activities can be considered: managing super news by indicating the most important innovation is forthcoming by our company; specially emphasizing the corporate name as being something very special; generating brand preference by indicating the company's brands being superior; and emphasizing the company's being always at the cutting edge by emphasizing how the company, its brands, and its products are proactive. Unfortunately, many companies consider promotional communications an expense item rather than a major investment that needs to be cultivated continuously.

Winning the communications war is not possible without successfully participating in the technology or R&D war, which has been discussed in many different ways throughout the book. But pricing the product to move it, in other words, the price war, must also be considered. Again, this topic is out of the constraints of this book; however, suffice it to say that if we cannot price the product for the greatest outreach in the market, we cannot possibly establish any competitive advantage, which is primarily based on generating consumer value.

Pricing practice must be such that it yields optimal market power by generating maximum consumer value and furthest possible reach in the market.[5] Generating consumer value by pricing strategically is unfortunately not the typical thinking or practice in many companies. Maximizing or attempting to maximize profits does not generate the optimal market power, which is the necessary ingredient of success and superiority in the market place for a prolonged period of time.

Here many American companies may provide extra service at the expense of more competitive pricing. However, the Japanese, on the other hand, would pass additional services along with lower prices. One such service is what Drucker[6] coins *knowledge worker*. Knowledge workers not only identify and analyze chaotic trends but also expand the firm's outreach.

Chaotic Trends Mean New Opportunities

In recent years, more advanced companies have developed an organizational unit combined of knowledge workers. Although it varies in terms of size, shape, sophistication, and reach and certainly the company's needs and orientation, one of the most important tasks of knowledge workers, this author firmly believes, is understanding and interpreting market changes in terms of possible opportunities for the firm, and operationalizing this belief by generating or modifying the firm's existing products and services.

Other Responsibilities for Knowledge Workers

As the complexity of many high-tech products increases and the level of sophistication of the prospective customers advances, reliance on knowledge workers will increase dramatically. As the company's sales force contacts prospective customers with unusual and complicated problems, the sales force will seek the help of knowledge workers who, in turn, will offer alternative solutions to the problem at hand. Thus, knowledge workers function as *information generators* as well as *decision facilitators*. It is critical to reiterate the fact that information workers first and foremost generate the necessary information for the corporate entity. But they also make the necessary information available where and when it is needed. As such, the importance of information workers' role cannot be overstated.

Information Is Not a Technology

It is almost strange in this age of high-tech and superversatile information technology that many people equate technology with information. Certainly better technology would provide better, more sensitive, and revealing data, but data are data and not information. There is a fine line between data and information. Data have to be *processed, interpreted*, and *converted* into corporate needs and corporate use. Then and only then, data become information, but again in this day and age of high technology, user-friendly techniques of data analyses and technologies are simply just that, user-friendly. But user-friendly does not mean decision-maker friendly.[7] The more user-friendly the products of high technology, the less decision-maker friendly they become. Thus, dealing with the information needs of the company, information workers have an extremely important task of generating not user friendly but decision-maker friendly information. In developing a major counterchaos strategy, decision-maker friendly information is the key necessary element.

Developing Dramatically New Products Is an Important Way of Controlling the Market

As was discussed in Chapters 7 and 9, developing dramatically new products is winning the technology war. This requires major commitment to the R&D activities of the firm and a substantial degree of staying power, since major breakthroughs do not emerge overnight.

In developing major new products Samli[8] talks about two major approaches: *convergence* and *divergence*. As the cable and telephone industries converge into one megaindustry information entertainment, goods, and services are brought to people's homes and offices. Thus, new paradigms are created, which should bring about totally new markets and new desirable products. This is how, for instance, hybrid cars using both electricity and gasoline came about. This is illustrated in Figure 13.1.

As convergence takes place it leads further in the direction of originality. Instead of narrow-minded industry-based strategy making, companies may find it necessary to form totally new paradigms. These are based on thinking beyond company, industry, and other boundaries. Obviously it was not converging manual calculators and electricity that gave the start to

Figure 13.1.
Developing Convergence.

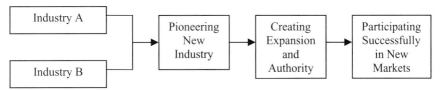

Source: Adapted and revised from Samli (2004).

the computer industry. Similarly the fuel cell driven cars are not part of con-
verged electricity and gasoline. Thus divergence may indicate a more major
development and more substantive inventions leading to a more powerful
leadership in an emerging major industry. This process is illustrated in
Figure 13.2.

THE FIVE COMPONENTS OF COUNTERCHAOS STRATEGY

Decision maker-friendly information is a necessary ingredient of a counterchaos strategy, but not sufficient of itself. Constructing five components
of such a strategy may make it sufficient. These components are: detection,
conversion, evaluation, facilitation, and implementation.

Based on our discussion thus far throughout this book, constructing a
counterchaos marketing strategy model is the zenith of our total activity.
The particular model presented here indicates a five-prong approach to
constructing a counterchaos marketing strategy.

Figure 13.2.
Developing Divergence.

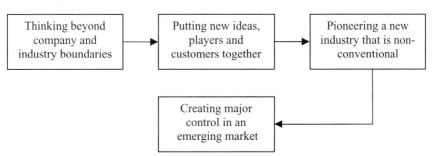

Detection

Detection of early symptoms of radical development in the market place is one of the themes of this book. It has been discussed to a certain extent in Chapter 4. Although it has been maintained that all firms must have a detection system based on the symptomatology of market turbulences, when market turbulences reach chaotic proportions, the early detection process must not only be activated but must also be accelerated further. This is the only way the outcome can be converted into new market opportunities. If the detection process is not accelerated, by the time the firm recognizes the newly emerging market opportunities, it will be too late.

Conversion

Conversion deals with interpreting the chaotic influences into new market opportunities. For instance, when Kodak faces a chaotic change in photography as the whole process moves in the direction of the disruptive technology of digital photography, instead of fighting a battle to remain in the conventional photography, it can easily enter a new competition of developing better digital cameras. Thus the threat through disruption becomes an opportunity through conversion.[9] It means the actual process, because of early detected opportunities, is converted into new realities. This process entails reassessment of market potentials and examining newly emerging gaps in the market. How would chaotic changes manifest themselves and what are the opportunities, or the new gaps, which would emerge from them? Obviously, here, imagination, improvisation, and prediction are the most critical tools for success.

Facilitation

Facilitation means creating an ongoing dialog between management and workers (democratization of the whole process) about rapidly changing conditions, what new key competencies are required, and how the company plans to respond. This is necessary for the management to generate support from its workers for its unexpected and sudden actions.

Evaluation

Evaluation implies valuing the radical changes that the firm is proposing on the basis of the changes in the market and their prioritization. This

Figure 13.3.
The Key Aspects of a Counterchaos Strategy.

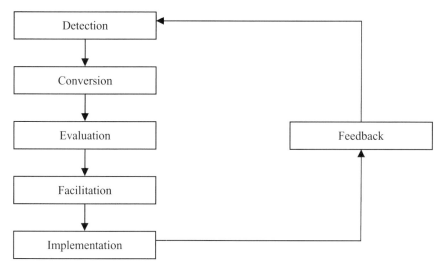

whole activity leads to generating or improving the contingency plans or revising the existing plan if not totally radical plans are proposed or are operationalized. Here, as discussed in different sections of this book, improvisation may be extremely handy in generating contingency plans. An energy company, say BP or Shell, must have other serious plans beyond petroleum to generate energy for the society and compete with others in the marketplace.

Implementation

Finally, implementation is really based on the above four phases of the overall plan. It spells out the characteristics of the proposed plan and how it is going to be materialized. Naturally this phase includes feedback as illustrated in Figure 13.3. Feedback here examines the differences between the planned and actual results so fast that some things can be done swiftly about the chaotic influences before it is too late. If the planned action does not perform well, this feedback adjustment mechanism becomes essential. However, even if the planned action works, there would be many ways to improve it further. Here, again, feedback is critical to understand the ways to improve the planned action.

MANAGING INFORMATION VERSUS BEING MANAGED BY IT

All decisions are based on some type of information. If that information is not managed well, it will not be proactive leading to viable decisions. Managing information well begins with generating powerful data.[10] Only powerful data is the type, kind, and quality of data that would enable the firm to fulfill its proactivity aspirations. If the data are not reliable or are not properly interpreted, then poor, unreliable, and misleading information will be generated. Thus, if the information is not well managed, poor information would mislead the company, which, in essence, would mean it is managing the company. Some 50 years after the introduction and failure of the Ford Edsel, which is a classic textbook story, it can easily be said that the company was misled by poor information, which resulted in a disaster.

FUTURE OUTLOOK

Generating and using good information are not natural activities. It is important that company researchers and knowledge workers clearly understand the decision makers' needs. Needless to say, the decision makers must know how to use that information. These important points require much thinking, interaction, and work on the part of all parties involved. Without such efforts and cooperation, the company will fail to generate consumer value.

THE VALUE CHAIN MUST BE FULLY FUNCTIONAL

In a market system such as ours, which is becoming more hypercompetitive, generating consumer value becomes job one. Not only is competition becoming more sophisticated and keener, but consumers are also becoming more demanding, more knowledgeable, and more sophisticated.

The flow of goods and services from maker or manufacturer to the end user or consumer must be not only smooth and going in the right direction, but also must be truly a value chain where, as proximity to the market narrows, the consumer value generated by this flow increases. Thus, our firm is not only involved in R&D or technology warfare, pricing warfare, or communication warfare, but is also involved in a very critical logistics warfare. More on this topic will be presented in Chapter 14; however, it must be reiterated that if the firm can develop the most appropriate strategy for itself and be successfully engaged in the wars previously mentioned, it will not only establish market superiority but it will also generate consumer value. Consumer value is the ultimate goal that rewards all our efforts to participate in the wars of hypercompetition. Hence, the firm is less vulnerable to chaotic influences.

CRITICAL COUNTERCHAOS CHECKLIST

1. What do we really know about our market and our customers?
2. Do we understand that in essence the market is a complex communication network?
3. Do we know how to detect emerging niche markets?
4. Can we win the R&D war, the communication war, and the pricing war?
5. Do we have adequate knowledge workers that would make a difference for us?

SUMMARY

This chapter deals with our ultimate goal, the market. It must be reiterated that if we don't know where we are going, we cannot get there. Markets are people who are willing and able to buy our products or services. The people are showing new trends that are opening up new opportunities under the broad title of new luxuries. However, the critical point is that in a market, any market, particularly in emerging new niche markets, there is a complex communication network in action. It is critical to enter into it successfully. This success partly requires the efforts of knowledge workers.

Managing information properly would enable the firm to construct an effective counterchaos strategy. This strategy has five components: detection, conversion, evaluation, facilitation, and implementation. Managing information is likely to become even more critical in the future because of the intensified hypercompetition prevailing in our markets. In order for the firm to establish market superiority and become counterchaotic, it must successfully participate in technology warfare, price warfare, communication warfare, and distribution warfare. These are essential ingredients of survival and success as the firm generates consumer value.

Chapter 14

Reaching the Markets

No matter how creative the company is, no matter how good its products or services, no matter how reasonable its prices, and no matter how good its communication system, if the firm cannot reach its target markets with its products and services, it cannot be successful in the market place. Since in recent years supply chain management has become an important focal issue and since in Chapter 11 we passingly discussed lean thinking from a rather negative perspective, this last chapter sets the record straight by emphasizing the important concept of supply chain referred to by many as the *value chain*.

LEAN THINKING

Particularly in mature markets where great increases in sales volumes are not expected to happen, improvements in the profit picture can materialize by cost cutting. Although, at least partially, this orientation gave birth to lean thinking strategy during the late 1970s and the early 1980s when there were deep recessions, cost cutting or managing by a bottom line has become a general orientation. In Chapter 11 this orientation is discussed as almost a tradition and playing a key role in the overall marketing activity of the firm. In essence this new "tradition" has brought about a conflict between the marketing activities and financial considerations within the firm.

The possible conflict between finance and marketing needs to be resolved if the firm wants to establish market superiority and become at least somewhat immune to chaotic market influences. In Drucker's profound words:[1] "Enterprises are paid to create wealth, not to control costs." This author very firmly believes in the premise that would establish proactive marketing orientation first and lean thinking second. Thus a major issue arises: just what is the place and the role of lean thinking in today's hypercompetitive markets?

How Lean Is Lean?

Since leanness or cost cutting is the total opposite of proactive aggressive market behavior, it is extremely difficult to determine how far the firm should go into cost cutting. Since finances, costs, and expenses are all internal accounting-related activities, they represent too much the path of least resistance. The greatest mistake in this whole process is that cost cutting is done against the current market position of the firm. Certainly if we can achieve or maintain the same market position with a much lower level of expenditures, this proposition becomes very attractive, and indeed in the very short run, this may be accomplished. However, the assumption that our market position can easily be achieved or maintained is a deadly proposition. Invariably as the firm tries to become leaner, something has got to give. If the sales force is reduced, or the advertising budget is scaled down, or the R&D outlays are limited and the like, any and all of these measures directly or indirectly have a major impact on the sales volume and market power of the firm. Thus leanness and proactive marketing are enemies. It is *extremely* critical that an optimal combination of the two be established. This is, unfortunately, against the practices of most firms, since marketing people and finance people in corporate entities first and foremost see only their own turf in the short run and are not adequately interactive.

Lean versus Agility

As the company thinks and plans the distribution systems for its products, it becomes clear that it must construct and manage a multitalented supply chain. The supply chain, above all, must deliver the firm's products to the target market efficiently and on time. Certainly, in this whole process, leanness is welcome; however, it does not direct the process on the basis of cost cutting. The process must fulfill the company's goal of delivering value to the consumer first and foremost. Although in supply chain literature, it is used in a somewhat different context, agility from the perspective of this author means the ability of the supply chain to make the necessary adjustments if and when market conditions change noticeably or dramatically, while products are within the chain and moving in the direction of the target market.

VALUE CHAINS DO NOT MEAN AGILITY FIRST

The process of moving the merchandise is extremely critical. After all, if the company cannot deliver the products it either has sold or is planning to sell, there is no finality to the exchange process on which the business in the market system thrives. The exchange process of delivering consumer value in return for a reward named profit has not been completed.

Perhaps the standard definition of supply chain management is critical here:

Supply Chain Management is the integration of key business processes from end user through original suppliers that provides products, services, and information that add value for customers and other stakeholders.[2]

By definition supply chains are value chains because they generate and disseminate consumer value. Supply chains, as seen from the above definition, are involved in two major groups of activities: First, upstream activities or generating products; and second, downstream activities disseminating products. In both cases, timing, physical handling, storing, and movement of materials or products are critical, but this author believes that supply chain management is very essential for the firm in managing the present, without which the firm cannot survive, rather than the future. This becomes a critical element of corporate strategic management because some supply chain scholars think that supply chain management supersedes all of the business activities. Therein lie at least two extremely important problems. First, the actual generation and dissemination of products constitute such overwhelming current activities that they hardly allow futuristic and proactive planning in the form of innovation and futuristic portfolios. Thus, an overemphasis on the supply chain is likely to interfere with managing the future.

Second, because of the very serious cost implications and extensive cost cutting orientations of many American businesses, supply chain management leads in the direction of what is called in Chapter 3 "too much management" by a bottom line rather than for a bottom line, which clearly creates a conflict between *market power generation* and *cost consciousness*, preventing the implementation of the Gretzky Rule of "we must go where the puck is likely to be" (Chapter 2). Perhaps stated very wisely by Collins,[3] "Good is the enemy of great," or *good supply chain management may interfere with great market superiority*. Market superiority is proactive, taking risk with the unknown and managing the future, whereas supply chain management is, indeed has to be, present oriented, reactive, and cost-conscious. Agility is defined as "using market knowledge and virtual corporation to exploit profitable opportunities in a volatile market place."[4] This extremely broad definition, if applied literally to supply chain management, would imply that the supply chain does all the managing for the future and the present. It excludes strategic management and counterchaos marketing. These are extremely critical issues to be ignored or arbitrarily decided based upon the personal biases of the participants in the management planning for market superiority. If a narrower concept of agility (or flexibility) were to be taken, then it is reasonable to say that the value chain will first target the market, handle the merchandise, cut cost, and be agile in doing all of these. Agility here will be reacting quickly and effectively to unforeseen problems in the distribution system. For example, as a mad cow scare emerges, how the beef supply chain management reacts is, from this author's point of view, a powerful example of the needed agility of the system in managing the present. But, it must be reiterated that merchandise handling is first, and agility is second.

LOGISTICS WARS AND MARKET SUPERIORITY

The larger the sales volume, the smaller the profit margins and, therefore, the more attractive it is to be able to cut costs. Thus, in attempts to establish market superiority, logistics wars are very much a part of the picture. Even if the company's products and services are not much different from those of competitors, being able to reach the right market on time with the right products is what the value chain does. The closer the products get to the target market, the greater the consumer value of products. Here again, supply chain scholars believe that demand can be managed. Without getting into conceptual semantics, this author believes that it is not managing the demand, but detecting it accurately and responding to it swiftly that would win the logistics wars.

CONSUMER VALUE GENERATION

If customer needs are satisfied properly and in time, the firm is managing the present well. Without prioritizing the wars that go on in the hypercompetitive markets, it is clear, for instance, that Wal-Mart or Dell cannot compete as effectively as they do without their very efficient and effective supply chain management.

Consumer Value versus Logistics Superiority

In the above examples of Dell and Wal-Mart, consumer value and logistics superiority are intricately tied together. Since both of the companies are volume players, their success, by definition, implies consumer value generation. However, there are many companies that are not volume players. Clearly other strategic weapons, such as product mix, promotion, price, and the like, may play a much more important role in generating consumer value than logistics. Generating consumer value implies market power or vice-versa.

Could Value Generation Eliminate Adversities?

In the market system, all firms are in the business of generating consumer value. Directly or indirectly, intentionally or unintentionally, all firms generate value; those who don't cease being in existence. The critical point here is that those who can generate more value than others get rewarded accordingly. At the writing of this book Wal-Mart is creating much more consumer value than K-Mart, and Target more than Sears. It can be stated, therefore, that counteracting market adversities or chaotic influences can be encountered by generating consumer value. This is achieved by winning the variety of market wars with some deviations of current practices or responding to market changes with disruptive new practices that generate consumer value by changing the rules of existing competition. In either case, the business cannot look at the future as a continuation of present or continue its practices in a "business as usual" manner.

LEAGILITY CAN BE AN ANSWER

Leanness and agility, "leagility,"[5] are two features that need to be balanced. Certainly reaching our markets in a lean manner is desirable and being agile in that process so that the company's outreach is not hindered is even better. When the problem emerges is when leanness takes over. It is much easier for a corporate entity that is having financial difficulties to lay off workers, close down factories, or move them down south of the border. In the short run this is doable, but with serious long-run implications. For

Figure 14.1.
The Supply Chain Influencers.

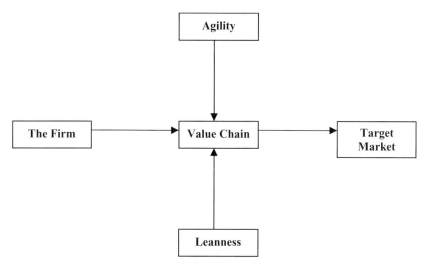

an executive who is making over $100 million a year to hold on to his job for one more year is important, and a stop-gap measure of laying off, say, 10,000 workers may simply accomplish this. But the future of the company can easily be jeopardized in this way. Laying off people, and closing down plants can easily reduce the market power of the firm. But above all, it is the orientation, the market adversities, or the chaotic problems that must be resolved by market-oriented solutions and not by simplistic financial ploys. Thus, leanness is extremely important to create consumer value and market power and is rather a poor choice to solve serious market problems.

Agility, on the other hand, is applicable not only to the value chain or logistics of the firm. It can be stretched to apply to counterchaos or nonconventional ways of thinking. It is not a simple financial ploy of laying off people or giving pay cuts to workers and the like. Rather, it means, in the broadest sense, the proactive orientation of the firm and the ability to respond to the accelerating market adversities quickly and effectively.

Thus, if we were to think "leagility," it would be extremely critical to determine the dimensions of leanness and agility. It is possible, for instance, to suffer from excessive agility and lose one's discipline, which Collins[6] considers to be of utmost importance for success. Figure 14.1 illustrates the two supply chain influencers, namely agility and leanness. These two have a very critical role to play in reaching the firm's markets.

BENCHMARKING AND THE HALO EFFECT

As is discussed earlier in the chapter, a learning organization can establish a sustainable competitive advantage. An important market-based learning activity is benchmarking, which is a structured process through which the firm establishes and tries to replicate "best practices" to generate and enhance its market power.[7]

In such a benchmarking activity at least eight marketing capabilities are identified: product or service development processes, generating optimal revenue by pricing, establishing and maintaining channels of distribution, communicating with the target market, selling to target customers by generating customer orders, managing market information as the firm learns about its markets, planning its marketing activity by generating marketing strategies, and finally, implementing these marketing strategies by planning resource deployments.[8]

Such a series of critical marketing prowess and capabilities however raises a critical question: whether benchmarking must be in the direction of managing the present versus the future. Here of course it is assumed that present and future are not the same and in fact they may not at all go in the same direction. It is quite conceivable that in the chaotic markets within which the firm functions, the present benchmarking is not likely to be adequate or even remotely applicable to the future's unexpected shocks that are almost commonplace in these markets.

Standard benchmarking theory indicates determining marketing capabilities of the firm associated with superior business performance. By definition, this overall activity is an extension of the past into the future and does not necessarily indicate what needs to be done in case of emergence of chaotic market changes.

If the management is futuristic, and following the Gretzky principle, going where the market is going to be, it will be rather difficult, if not impossible, to benchmark. The fact that benchmarking deals with organizational learning that identifies the capabilities and practices related to superior market performance, by definition, becomes impossible since best practices in the chaotic new area are not known and therefore the resultant market position and profitability features of benchmarking cannot be established. If GM decides to put a major effort in fuel cell cars, it will be rather difficult for the company to identify benchmarking activity based on best practices. They are not yet established. Figure 14.2 illustrates how benchmarking works. It also illustrates that benchmarking is more of an attempt to continue the program. The Figure begins with organizational learning. Knowledge in this case is converted into benchmarks that would

Figure 14.2.
Benchmarking and Market Performance.

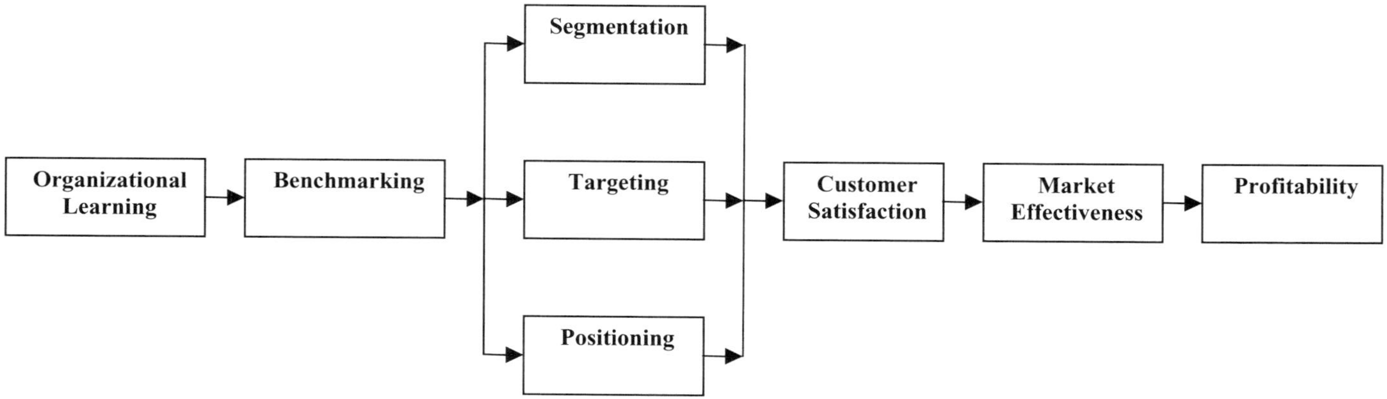

facilitate best practices in segmenting, targeting, and positioning. If the best practices lead in the customer satisfaction then the firm establishes its market power, which leads to profitability but also development of a halo effect. Because of its market power the firm is recognized and its halo would lead to successful introduction of new products and services. At the point of writing this book Target and Costco are two typical examples of market effectiveness or market power. Because they have established a halo effect they may be very successful in establishing new products or services. In this case it is critical to realize that the firm, while managing the present through its halo effect, may be insuring its future as well.

WHAT ABOUT IMPROVISATION?

Earlier, in Chapter 7, we discussed improvisation as a major defense activity against chaotic shock waves in the market. As Grove posits,[9] "sooner or later, something fundamental in your business world will change." Not only in modern markets such events are happening more often but also coming from outside in the form of shock waves. In such situations it is difficult to visualize how benchmarking can be implemented despite all good intentions. When Intel found itself being forced out of the "memory business" into "microprocessing," it is quite doubtful that its benchmarking efforts and the resultant benchmarks remained intact. The best practices that may have been understood and learned for the company's memory business activities are not likely to be applicable to its microprocessing businesses.

Here there are two separate issues to be considered: first was the move from memory business to microprocessing strictly a variation of current practices and hence it is the extension of the present, or was it where the company saw the market is likely to move as the puck in the Gretzky principle? Second, did the company use any improvisation-based scenarios?

Based on these two major inquiries, the most critical consideration here is that if the microprocessing business is significantly different than what the company primarily has been doing and if it is futuristic, then it would have been very effective to have improvisation scenarios dealing with this switch. It is even more critical to think that such an improvisation scenario has an important benchmarking model. In other words, the model presented in Figure 14.2 can be and in fact must be approximated for each and every viable improvisation scenario. Based on past experiences, imagination, and improvisation skills, best practices-based benchmarking can be approximated for each of the major improvisation scenarios. It must be reiterated that connecting benchmarking to improvisation is one of the most proactive marketing undertakings that would need to be explored carefully. In Figure 14.2 before every benchmarking activity there is the possibility of using an improvisation scenario. This is one of the major ways how the present and the future can be connected for success in chaotic markets.

If the firm is likely not to have a smooth continuity between the present and the future because of the unexpected shock waves in the chaotic markets, it must resort to some measures that would keep the name of the company or some of its family brands alive and powerful. In other words the company may move from memory business to microprocessing, or, say, from electricity generation to consumer financing the corporate name and/or the corporate brand can be kept general and powerful enough that the major switch in the core activities of the firm can easily be accepted by the market.

CONNECTING PRESENT TO FUTURE

Throughout this book we discussed managing the company in the present time and connecting it to the future. Here we have argued that future is not an extension of the present. In fact it is in the company's best interest to invent its own future or in other words go where the puck is likely to be located.

If a company is successful in managing the present and hence is generating market power, it has two very important indications of power. It has a well known and respected corporate image and equally or even better known brand equity. Names such as IBM, Coca-Cola, Mitsubishi, and the like are very strong indicators of market power. When such market power indicators are present it becomes easier to introduce new products or services even though these products and services are not part of the company's existing product or service activities. It is possible for instance for General Electric (GE) to introduce a new electric car. This would be acceptable by the market because the GE name or the logo is broad enough and has a halo effect. Generating a halo effect through the firm's market power is certainly compatible with going where the puck is going to be indicated by chaotic market shocks. All firms, as they thrive to establish market power by generating consumer value, must develop a corporate image and/or a brand image that will provide a halo effect and connect the present to the future even if the future is not a continuation of the present activities and the status of the firm.

INTERMEDIATE BRANDS

While IBM, Coca-Cola, and the like are very strong indicators of market power that connects their present to the future, there are intermediate brands that need to establish market power. Many companies have products or services that are not strictly an end product. For example, Intel (the major chip-maker in the world) has a Pentium brand but does not appear in the finished product, which is the personal computer. The company produced processors much faster and more efficiently and did very well in this narrow-focused competition. However, gaining brand power would make the company more versatile in terms of introducing other product parts or ingredients. Thus the company needs intermediate brands (or ingredient brands) that will enable the company to future and will make it much more chaos-resistant. At the time of writing of this book Intel is in the process of generating three new intermediate brands: Viiv to be used for home PC, Centrino to be used for notebooks, and Core to be used as a dual core chip. Establishing ingredient brands is more difficult than regular consumer brand. The question here becomes: how much emphasis on consumer information and how much information for the maker of the finished product? Again, at the time of writing of this book Intel is planning a $2.5 billion advertising and marketing blitz to cover both of these bases that may make the company more chaos resistant. It would improve its chances to enter emerging markets quickly.

GOOD PROFITS VERSUS BAD PROFITS

This book is based on the premise that if we generate consumer value we are also creating market power. However, there are those who, at least in the short-run, are making much money without creating consumer value. At the time of writing of this book petroleum companies are making obscene amounts of profits without generating consumer value. Exxon is paying $400 million bonus to its retiring CEO. There is, therefore, what Reichheld[10] calls bad profits. He maintains that companies can easily get hooked on these. Bad profits are not generating value but extracting value. Reichheld maintains that churn rates in cellular phones, credit cards, newspapers, cable TV, airlines, and many others have deteriorated to the point of companies losing half of their customers in less than 3 years implying that they are not very happy. Consumers who feel ignored or taken advantage of are likely to remember and get even. Companies have difficulty growing on bad profits. They cannot survive on "bad profits" for long and stay in business. If the company is attempting to connect the present and the future this can be achieved by "good profits." Both in the present and the future the proactive firm must generate "good profits" that are simultaneously creating consumer value. These are values that are earned with customers' enthusiastic cooperation because they are delighted and will come back for more. Furthermore, they will bring friends, colleagues, and acquaintances. Connecting present to future, therefore, requires generating good profits by delighting the consumers rather than generating bad profits.

CRITICAL COUNTERCHAOS CHECKLIST

1. Can we create wealth by generating consumer value?
2. Are we using value chains to our advantage?
3. Are we generating and enhancing our market power by replicating "best practices?"
4. As we know, sooner or later something fundamental in our business world is likely to change: can we really identify it?
5. If we can identify critical changes in our markets can we develop improvisation scenarios to cope with them?

SUMMARY

Reaching target markets is vital for the firm. Its distribution or its supply chain management is essential for survival and generation of consumer value. In this chapter, two special concepts are particularly emphasized. These are leanness and agility. In accomplishing what the supply chain should do, it must first aim and deliver the proper merchandise mix on time and at a low cost. From this perspective, leanness deals much more with managing the present rather than the future. Agility can be applied to all aspects of the firm's strategic posture. If it is treated that way, then it is an essential element of not only managing the present, but also the future.

Postscript

It must be reiterated that achieving market power is intimately related to generating consumer value, which is accomplished by applying the Gretzky principle successfully. Throughout this book numerous examples are given as to how to achieve market power and improve the company's chances to survive. We have not necessarily sought greatness but surely we have enhanced our chances for survival.

The essence of this book is depicted in Figure P.1. Its overall orientation is implementing the Gretzky principle and go to where the market will be rather than where it is. It starts with identification of chaos-causing factors in the market. It moves on to the firm's ability to perceive possible chaotic events. It becomes necessary to prioritize these events and their possible opportunity-generating characteristics. Here, if the firm is a learning organization, it has a better chance to understand the situation in a more realistic manner. A learning organization can detect the forthcoming chaotic shock wave that the market may be about to present. Hence such a learning organization can manage chaotic shock waves before they play havoc on the company's well being. As the firm implements its strategic plans and chaos-causing factors enter the picture, it becomes extremely critical to be able to determine where the market will be. Here, paying particular attention to emerging disruptive technologies can play a critical role in the firm's attempts to generate consumer value and survive. It becomes inevitable for the firm to improvise since at this point it is traveling in uncharted territories. Evaluation of its generic strategy also becomes critical here. After all, without a strategy to survive today there will not be a tomorrow. Once the firm has an idea as to where the market is likely to be, it will let its drive to innovate become totally

Figure P.1.
Achieving Market Power In A Bird's-Eye View.

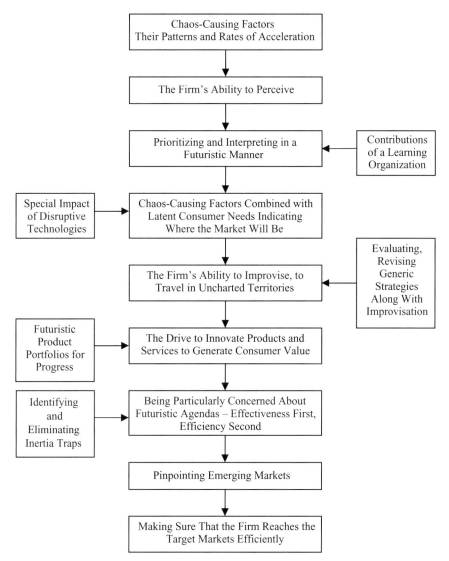

active. It will generate not only new products or services for the market as it changes, but it will also develop a futuristic portfolio of products and services. The firm understands that, without effectiveness in successfully reaching its target markets, efficiency becomes rather useless. Here the firm must also be able to pinpoint emerging new markets and reach them efficiently.

A 12-point strategic agenda can be considered as a natural outcome of this book. It is clearly the road map to achieving market power.

1. Do Not Ignore Chaos

   Throughout this book, it has been argued that markets are hypercompetitive and very changeable. Hence, ignoring chaos-causing factors and chaotic influences is not only poor marketing but does not enhance the company's market position or competitive powers. Understanding how market forces influence our company is essential for survival.

2. Be Proactive

   The importance of proactivity in managing possible chaos cannot be overstated. The modern company cannot simply live in the shadow of corporate culture that extends present practices rather than proactivity. Successful companies must try to be market drivers as opposed to be market driven in at least by using some of their product and service offerings and hence generating market power.

3. Present versus the Future

   All firms live and function in the present, but those that are powerful and immune to extreme market adversities manage the future. Managing the future has been advocated throughout this book as the key to establish market power or even market leadership. Again, this may mean attempting and succeeding in being a market driver rather than being driven by the market.

4. Change Your Corporate Culture

   A futuristic corporate culture is a deliberate orientation that needs to be cultivated. Free of conventional wisdom, such a culture has a drive to innovate. Such a corporation is a learning organization and undertakes a lot of improvisation. Since shock waves cannot be predicted in total accuracy, the skills to improvise must be sharpened.

5. Innovate, Innovate, Innovate

   Being the innovator and taking advantage of being the first mover are important considerations. The firm must pursue not only incremental product development policies, but also particularly radical product development policies. As such, the firm must have a futuristic portfolio so that if and when needed, it can generate new products swiftly.

6. Understand Where the Future Opportunities Are

   Tracking megatrends, determining where the emerging markets are and evaluating where the major threats are coming from, are all critical for establishing market superiority and chaos immunity. Being proactive and going after future opportunities are necessities for achieving market power.

7. Use Your Strengths

    The firm not only must know its core competencies but also must be able to assess the necessary changes in these core competencies, as it engages in radical product development as well as in changing the rules of competition. Here and throughout the total process, the firm must know that there are always inertia traps. They block progress and interfere with proper utilization of the firm's core competencies.

8. Think Out of the Box

    Exercise and cultivate vision and values in a disciplined manner and get away from traditions. Democratize your people to become part of managing the future process. Incumbency may be good, but certainly works against the greatness that can be achieved by thinking out of the box. Ambidextrousity in managing the present and the future is advocated throughout this book.

9. Emphasize What We Should Be Doing

    Being futuristic and unleashing creativity to manage the future not only immunizes the firm against shocking chaotic events but also establishes market power, even when chaotic conditions or extreme adversities do not exist. To be sure such preemptive orientation pays off in the future.

10. Develop and Follow a Generic Strategy

    If we don't know where we are going, we cannot get there. Out of nine generic strategies suggested in this book, the most suitable one for the company is likely to immunize it against unexpected chaotic influences. This may mean some variation or some combination of these strategies. But, above all, it means managing the present and the future in a creative and balanced manner.

11. Understand What Your Markets Are

    Without understanding the markets well and being intimately involved in them, the company cannot generate consumer value, which comes with market power. Such an understanding would facilitate the development and implementation of a counterchaos strategy. Again, this means going to where the puck is likely to be rather than where the puck is.

12. Reach Out to Markets

    Your products must reach the right market at the right time. Managing the supply chain is a very complex task. In managing the distribution of your products, you must consider leanness and agility, but above all, must make sure that the whole activity is aimed at the right market. In essence, effectiveness is first and efficiency is second. Sending the wrong products to the wrong markets efficiently is hardly desirable. Once again, these 12 key points may not make us great, but they are likely to enhance our chances of survival and success.

Figure P.2.
A Research Agenda.

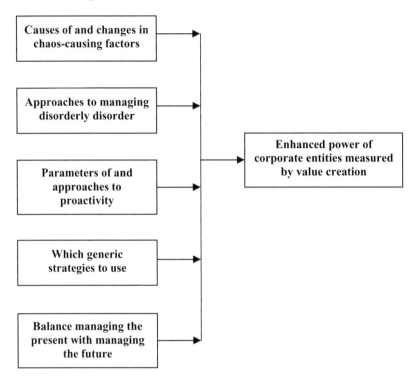

A FUTURE RESEARCH AGENDA

Almost all of the ideas and positions presented throughout this book can be and should be researched further. Hence, this book itself is a research agenda. However, five key areas of research stand out (Figure P.2). These are briefly discussed as follows.

Causes of and Changes in Chaos-Causing Factors

No research is sufficient to enhance the corporate sensitivity to emerging or changing chaotic market conditions. The corporate entity must develop an extremely sensitive system of not only detecting danger but also understanding how such emerging or changing chaotic factors would mean opportunities for the firm. Again, going by the principle that *we may not get a second chance to make a first impression,* the firm must learn to accelerate the counterchaos strategy presented in Chapter 13. Detection, conversion, evaluation, facilitation, and implementation (Figure 13.1) are all research-based phenomena. Putting them all together swiftly would call for not only serious emphasis on the chaos phenomena per se, but also on strategic adjustment that be must pursued immediately.

Approaches to Managing Disorderly Disorder

Much research is needed to determine how the firm can use the Gretzky Principle, that is, discovering the best way to find itself not where the market is but where the market is going to be. The research effort that is needed in this context is the continuation of the first item in this research agenda. Understanding the causes of and the changes in chaos-causing factors is essential in generating counterchaos strategies. However, in general terms, research can reveal that there are (or at least there should be) certain general game plans that may immunize our firm against unexpected and chaotic developments in the market place. Since one of the themes throughout this book has been "disorderly disorder," approaches toward such a phenomenon are not at all similar to approaches that may be used to a phenomenon that may be described as "orderly disorder." Since disorderly disorder takes place in the short-run and can be devastating, the corporate entity cannot wait to see some kind of an order emerging from the existing disorder. The firm will not have such a luxury of wait and see. Here, in order to cope with disorderly disorder, the firm's research emphasis may be on improvisation, agility, and core competency areas, among others.

Parameters of an Approach to Proactivity

One of the key issues throughout this book has been the conflict between managing the present versus managing the future. Certainly, this is a very critical area. In order to be at least somewhat immune to the accelerating environmental adversities, it has been maintained in this book that being proactive and being futuristic are critical. The key research question arises: Just how much emphasis on the present and how much emphasis on the future? How do we identify the details of these two, and how much ambidextrousity can we afford to have?

Which Generic Strategy To Use?

Again, one of the themes of this book has been that if the firm has adequate market power, it is reasonably protected against market adversities.

Using an appropriate generic strategy is creating market power. The question arises just which strategy option should be used and why? Research not only must be able to provide information that would enable the company to choose the best strategy, but also indicate when it may be modified or even abandoned.

Present or Future?

Which generic strategy to use leads the company to think about how much emphasis must be put on the present and how much on the future. Without the present there will be no future, but without the future there won't be anything. Thus the proper ratio between balancing the present (marketing management emphasis) and the future (the strategic planning orientation) needs to be established. This book primarily deals with the latter and proposes that a company should be at the cutting edge of the market and be ready for the unexpected from the market any time. Much research is needed in determining how this readiness can be enhanced.

Notes

PREFACE

1. Jim Collins (2001), *Good to Great*, New York: Harper Business.
2. Ibid.
3. Ibid.

INTRODUCTION

1. A. Coskun Samli (2002), *In Search of Equitable, Sustainable Globalization*, Westpoint, CT: Quorum Books.
2. Thomas Friedman (2002), *The Lexus and the Olive Tree*, New York: Anchor Books.
3. A. Coskun Samli (1993), *Counterturbulence Marketing*, Westpoint, CT: Quorum Books.
4. Clayton M. Christensen (2003), *The Innovator's Dilemma*, New York: Harper Business Essentials.
5. Ibid.
6. Nicholas D. Evans (2003), *Business Innovations and Disruptive Technologies*, Upper Saddle River, NJ: Financial Times-Prentice Hall; Christensen 2003, op cit.
7. Peter F. Drucker (1980), *Managing In Turbulent Times*, p. 4, New York: Harper and Row.
8. Art Turock (2002), *Invent Business Opportunities No One Else Can Imagine*, Franklin Lakes, NJ: Career Press.
9. Samli (1993), op cit.
10. Samli (1993), op cit.

CHAPTER 1: THE CAUSES OF CHAOTIC PRESSURES

1. William Joyce, Nitin Nohria, and Bruce Roberson (2003), *What Really Works*, New York: Harper Business.
2. Peter F. Drucker (1980), *Managing In Turbulent Times*, New York: Harper and Row.
3. A. Coskun Samli (1993), *Counterturbulence Marketing*, Westport, CT: Quorum Books.
4. Clayton M. Christensen (2003), *The Innovator's Dilemma*, New York: Harper Business Essentials.
5. Ibid.
6. Brynn Hibbert and Ian F. Wilkinson (1994), "Chaos Theory and the Dynamics of Marketing Systems," *Journal of Academy of Marketing Science*, Summer, 218–233.
7. Andrew S. Grove (1999), *Only the Paranoid Survive*, p. 30, New York: Currency Books.
8. A. Coskun Samli (1985), *Technology Transfer*, Westport, CT: Greenwood.
9. Steve Hamm (2006), "Is Your Company Fast Enough?" *Business Week*, March 27, 68–76.
10. Samli (1993), op cit.
11. Eric Schonfeld and Omd Malik (2003), "Gulp," *Business 2.0*, August, 90–95.
12. A. Coskun Samli (2006), "A Proactive Counterchaos Marketing Strategy: Survival and Success in a Turbulent Era," *Journal of Marketing Theory and Practice*, Fall, 315–322.
13. Christensen (2003), op cit.
14. Ibid.

CHAPTER 2: PAST STRATEGIES WERE GOOD, BUT . . .

1. Art Turock (2002), *Invent Business Opportunities*, Franklin Lakes, NJ: Career Press.
2. Donald N. Sull (2005), *Why Good Companies Go Bad*, Boston, MA: Harvard Business School.
3. Turock (2002), op cit.
4. John Kenneth Galbraith (1958), *The Affluent Society*, Boston: Houghton Mifflin Co.
5. Clayton M. Christensen (2003), *The Innovator's Dilemma*, New York: Harper Business Essentials.

CHAPTER 3: CONVENTIONAL WISDOM—NOT

1. Clayton M. Christensen (2003), *The Innovator's Dilemma*, New York: Harper Business Essentials.

2. John Kenneth Galbraith (1958), *The Affluent Society*, Boston: Houghton Mifflin Co.

3. Philip Kotler (2002), *Marketing Management*, Upper Saddle River, NJ: Prentice Hall.

4. Al Ries (1996), *Focus*, New York: Harper Business.

5. Ibid.

6. Theodore Levitt (1960), "Marketing Myopia," *Harvard Business Review*, July-August, 24–47.

7. Christensen (2003), op cit.

8. Andrew S. Grove (1999), *Only The Paranoid Survive*, New York: Currency Books.

9. Bruce Buskirk and Molly Lavik (2004), *Entrepreneurial Marketing*, Natorp, OH: Thomson, South-Western.

CHAPTER 4: EARLY PERFORMANCE ASSESSMENT AS A START

1. Louisa Wah (1998), "The Edge," *Management Review*, November, 25–29.

2. A. Coskun Samli (2006).

3. As discussed in Wah (1998), op cit.

4. Ibid.

5. Ibid.

6. Peter F. Drucker (1980), *Managing In Turbulent Times*, p. 42, New York: Harper and Row.

7. A. Coskun Samli (1993), *Counterturbulence Marketing*, Westport, CT: Quorum Books.

8. Samli (1993), op cit.

9. Drucker (1980), op cit.

CHAPTER 5: THE ROLE OF THE COUNTERCHAOS MARKETER

1. Louisa Wah (1998), "The Edge," *Management Review*, November, 25–29.

2. Andrew S. Grove (1999), *Only The Paranoid Survive*, New York: Currency Books.

3. Ibid.

4. Ibid.

5. Clayton M. Christensen (2003), *The Innovator's Dilemma*, New York: Harper Essentials.

6. A. Coskun Samli (1993), *Counterturbulence Marketing*, Westport, CT: Quorum Books.

7. A. Coskun Samli (2006), "Surviving in Chaotic Modern Markets: Strategic Considerations in Turbulent Times," *Journal of Marketing Theory and Practice*, Fall, 315–322.

CHAPTER 6: DEVELOPING A LEARNING ORGANIZATION

1. William Joyce, Nitin Nohria, and Bruce Roberson (2003), *What Really Works*, New York: Harper Business.
2. John Naisbitt (1982), *Megatrends*, New York: Warner Books.
3. Peter F. Drucker (1992), *Managing for the Future*, New York: Truman Talley Books; Peter F. Drucker (1999), *Management Challenges for the 21st Century*, New York: Harper Business.
4. A. Coskun Samli (1996), *Information-Driven Marketing Decisions*, Westport, CT: Quorum Books.
5. Ibid.
6. A. Coskun Samli and Scott Fisher (2003), "Organizational Learning As A Strategic Tool: Operationalizing An Index of Learning," *Development in Marketing Science*.
7. Jim Collins (2001), *Good to Great*, New York: Harper Business.

CHAPTER 7: THE ART AND SCIENCE OF IMPROVISATION

1. Ali E. Akgun and Gary S. Lynn (2002), "New Product Development Team Improvisation and Speed-to-Market: An Extended Model," *European Journal of Innovation Management*, 5(3), 117–129.
2. Emmett C. Murphy and Mark A. Murphy (2002), *Leading On The Edge of Chaos*, Paramus, NJ: Prentice Hall Press.
3. Steve Hamm (2006), "How Smart Companies are Creating New Products— and Whole New Businesses —Almost Overnight," *Business Week*, March 27, 68–76.
4. João Vieira daCunha (1999), "Improvisation in Global Virtual Terms," *Portugal E-mail*, Lisbon-Portugal.
5. Christian Chelariu, Wesley J. Johnston, and Louise Young, (2002), "Learning to Improvise, Improvise to Learn a Process of Responding to Complex Environments," *Journal of Business Research*, 55, 141–147.
6. Hamm (2006), op cit.

CHAPTER 8: PRODUCTS AND SERVICES IN GENERATING CONSUMER VALUE

1. A. Coskun Samli (1993), *Counterturbulence Marketing*, Westport, CT: Quorum Books.
2. P. Thomond and F. Lettice (2002), "Disruptive Innovation Explored," International Conference on Concurrent Engineering, Research and Applications, July, 25–28.
3. Ibid.
4. Louisa Wah (1998), "The Edge," *Management Review*, November, 25–29.
5. Samli (1993), op cit.
6. Ibid.
7. Ibid.

8. Ibid.

9. John Naisbitt (1982), *Megatrends*, New York: Warner Books.

10. Joseph B. Pine, II (1999), *Mass Customization*, Boston, MA: Harvard Business School Press.

11. Karl T. Ulrich and Steven D. Eppinger (2004), *Product Design and Development*, New York: McGraw-Hill/Irwin.

CHAPTER 9: THE DRIVE TO INNOVATE

1. Jin K. Han, Namwoon Kim, and Hong-Bumm Kim (2001), "Entry Barriers: A Dull One-, or Two-Edged Sword for Incumbents? Unraveling the Paradox From a Contingency Perspective," *Journal of Marketing*, January, 1–14.

2. Clayton M. Christensen (2003), *The Innovator's Dilemma*, New York: Harper Business Essentials.

3. Andrew S. Grove (1999), *Only the Paranoid Survive*, p. 68, New York: Currency Books.

4. Rajesh K. Chandy and Gerard J. Tellis (1998), "Organizing for Radical Product Innovation: The Overlooked Role of Willingness to Cannibalize," *Journal of Marketing Research*, November, 474–487.

5. Marion Debruyne, Rudy Moehaert, Abbie Griffin, Susan Hart, Eric J Hultink, and Henry Robben (2002), "The Impact of New Product Launch Strategies on Competitive Reaction in Industrial Markets," *Product Innovation Management*, 19, 159–170.

6. Ibid.

7. Rajshree Agarwal and Michael Gort (2001), "First-Mover Advantage and the Speed of Competitive Entry," *The Journal of Law and Economics*, April, 161–176.

8. Christensen (2003), op cit.

9. Geoffrey A. Moore, (1995), *Inside The Tornado*, New York: Harper Books.

10. William Joyce, Nitin Nohria, and Bruce Roberson (2003), *What Really Works*, New York: Harper Business.

11. A. Coskun Samli and Julie Ann E. Weber (2000), "A Theory of Successful Product Breakthrough Management: Learning from Success," *Journal of Product and Brand Management*, January, 35–55.

12. Michael J Silverstein and Neil Fiske (2005), *Trading Up*, New York: Penguin Group.

13. Ibid.

CHAPTER 10: USING ONE'S STRENGTHS

1. Peter Drucker (1954), *The Practice of Management*, New York: McGraw-Hill.

2. Al Ries (1996), *Focus*, New York: Harper Business.

3. George Stalk, Philips Evans, and Lawrence E. Shulman (1992), "Competing On Capabilities: The New Rules of Corporate Strategy," *Harvard Business Review*, March/April, 57–69.

4. A. Coskun Samli and Eric Shaw (2002), "Achieving Managerial Synergism: Balancing Strategic Business Units and Profit Centers," *Journal of Market Focused Management*, January, 59–73.

5. Amy V. Snyder and H. William Ebeling, Jr. (1992), "Targeting A Company's Real Core Competencies," *Journal of Business Strategy*, Nov/Dec, 26–32.

6. Geoffrey A. Moore (1995), *Inside the Tornado*, New York: Harper Business Books.

7. Andrew S. Grove (1999), *Only the Paranoid Survive*, New York: Currency Books.

8. Art Turock (2002), *Invent Business Opportunities No One Else Can Imagine*, Franklin Lakes, NJ: Career Press.

CHAPTER 11: BECAUSE WE HAVE BEEN DOING IT THIS WAY TRADITIONALLY

1. Jeffrey A. Rigsby and Guy Greco (2003), *Mastering Strategy*, New York: McGraw Hill.

2. Donald N. Sull (2005), *Why Good Companies Go Bad*, Boston, MA: Harvard Business School Press.

3. Louise Lee (2006), "It's Dell vs. The Dell Way," *Business Week*, March 6, 61–62.

4. Rigsby and Greco (2003), op cit.

5. Jim Collins (2001), *Good to Great*, New York: Harper Business.

6. Rigsby and Greco (2003), op cit.

7. James P. Womak and Daniel T. Jones (1996), *Lean Thinking*, New York: Simon and Schuster.

8. A. Coskun Samli (1993), *Counterturbulence Marketing*, Westport, CT: Quorum Books.

9. Ibid.

10. Michael J. Silverstein and Neil Fiske (2005), *Trading Up*, New York: Penguin Group.

11. Amy V. Snyder and William H. Ebeling, Jr. (1992), "Targeting a Company's Real Core Competencies," *Journal of Business Strategy*.

12. Mahen Tampoe (1994), "Exploiting the Core Competencies of Your Organization," *Long Range Planning*, August, 66–77.

CHAPTER 12: IT IS NOT WHAT THEY DO—IT IS WHAT WE SHOULD BE DOING

1. Art Turock (2002), *Invent Business Opportunities No One Else Can Imagine*, Franklin Lakes, NJ: Career Press.

2. Richard D'Aveni (1999), "Strategic Supremacy through Disruption and Dominance," *Sloan Management Review*, Spring, 127–135.

3. Turock (2002), op cit.

4. D'Aveni (1999), op cit.

5. Ibid.

6. Andrew S. Grove (1999), *Only The Paranoid Survive*, New York: Currency Books.

7. Turock (2002), op cit.

8. Michael J. Silverstein and Neil Fiske (2005), *Trading Up*, New York: Penguin Group.

9. Peter F. Drucker (1999), "Beyond the Information Revolution," p. 22, *The Atlantic Monthly*, October, 41–57.

10. Jim Collins (2001), *Good to Great*, New York: Harper Business.

11. Jack Trout (2004), *Trout on Strategy*, New York: McGraw-Hill.

12. A. Coskun Samli and James Wills (1989), "Global Computer Marketing Strategies," *Industrial Marketing Management*, November, 271–280.

13. Kenichi Ohmae (1982), *The Mind of the Strategist*, New York: Penguin.

14. Turock (2002), op cit., p. 43

15. Rick Page (2002), *Hope Is Not A Strategy*, New York: McGraw-Hill.

CHAPTER 13: WHAT ARE THOSE MARKETS ANYWAY?

1. A. Coskun Samli (1993), *Counterturbulence Marketing*, Westport, CT: Quorum Books.

2. Richard A. D'Aveni (1999), "Strategic Supremacy through Disruption and Dominance," *Sloan Management Review*, Spring, 127–135.

3. Michael J. Silverstein and Neil Fiske (2005), *Trading Up*, New York: Penguin Group.

4. Gerry Khermouch and Jeff Green (2001), "Buzz-Marketing," *Business Week*, July 30, 50–56.

5. Samli (1993), op. cit.

6. Peter F. Drucker (1999), "Beyond the Information Revolution," *The Atlantic Monthly*, October, 41–57.

7. A. Coskun Samli (1996), *Information Driven Marketing Decisions*, Westport, CT: Quorum Books.

8. A. Coskun Samli (2004), "Corporate Search for Market Power: The Seven Strategic Megatrends of the Twentieth Century," *Business and Society Review*, Summer, 263–280.

9. Clayton M Christensen and Michael E. Raynor (2003), *The Innovator's Solution*, Boston, MA: Harvard Business School Press.

10. Samli (1996), op cit.

CHAPTER 14: REACHING THE MARKETS

1. Peter F. Drucker (1999), *Management Challenges for the 21st Century*, New York: Harper Business.

2. Douglas M. Lambert and Martha C. Cooper (2000), "Issues in Supply Chain Management," *Industrial Marketing Management*, 29, 65–83.

3. Jim Collins (2001), *Good to Great*, New York: Harper Business.

4. Ben J. Naylor, Mohamed M. Naim, and Danny Berry (1999), "Leagility: Integrating the Lean and Agile Manufacturing Paradigms in the Total Supply Chain," *Production Economics*, 62, 107–118.

5. Ibid.

6. Collins (2001), op cit.

7. Douglas W. Voorhies and Neil A. Morgan (2005), "Benchmarking Marketing Capabilities for Sustainable Competitive Advantage," *Journal of Marketing*, January, 80–94.

8. Ibid.

9. Andrew Grove (1999), *Only the Paranoid Survive*, quote from XIII, New York: Currency Books.

10. Fred Reichheld (2006), *The Ultimate Question*, Boston, MA: Harvard Business School Press.

Index

About the Author

DR. A. COSKUN (JOSH) SAMLI is Research Professor of Marketing and International Business at the University of North Florida.

Dr. Samli received his bachelor's degree from Istanbul Academy of Commercial Sciences. His MBA is from the University of Detroit and his Ph.D. is from Michigan State University. As a Ford Foundation Fellow, he has done postdoctoral work at UCLA and at the University of Chicago, as well as an International Business Program Fellow at New York University.

In 1974–1975 he was Sears-AACSB Federal Faculty Fellow in the Office of Policy and Plans, U.S. Maritime Administration. In 1983, Dr. Samli was invited to New Zealand as the Erskine Distinguished Visiting Scholar to lecture and undertake research at Canterbury University. In 1985, Dr. Samli was a Fulbright Distinguished Lecturer in Turkey. He was selected as the Beta Gamma Sigma, L. J. Buchan Distinguished Professor for the academic year 1986–1987. He was given a research fellowship by the Center of Science Development, South Africa, in February 1995. He was awarded a fellowship by the Finnish Academy of Sciences for a lecture in the Doctoral Seminar, June 1999.

Dr. Samli is the author or coauthor of more than 250 scholarly articles, 17 books, and 30 monographs. Dr. Samli has been invited, as a distinguished scholar, to deliver papers in many parts of the world by many universities. He has lectured extensively in Europe, Eastern Europe, Middle East, Far East, Oceania, and many other parts of the world. He has been very active in the Fulbright Commission. Dr. Samli is on the review board of seven major journals. He was the first president and a research fellow of the International Society for Quality of Life Studies (ISQOLS).

Dr. Samli is a Distinguished Fellow in the Academy of Marketing Science and a past chairman of its Board of Governors. He has done some of the earlier studies on the poor, elderly, and price discrimination. His most recent books are *Social Responsibility in Marketing* (1992) published by Quorum; *International Marketing: Planning and Practice* (1993) published by McMillan; *Counterturbulence Marketing* (1993) published by Quorum; *International Consumer Behavior* (1995) published by Quorum; *Information Driven Marketing Decisions* (1996) published by Quorum; *Recent Developments in Marketing QOL Research* (1996) published by Quorum; *Marketing Globally* (1998) published by NTC; *Marketing Strategies for Success in Retailing* published by Quorum (1998); and *Empowering the American Consumer* published by Quorum (2001). His books like *Entering and Succeeding in Third World Countries*, by Thomson (2004), *Up against the Retail Giants*, by Thomson (2005), *Social Responsibility in Marketing*, and *Empowering the American Consumer* were considered among the most important academic books in the United States by the *Choice* magazine, which is managed by librarians. These books received the *Choice* award. Praeger is publishing his eighteenth book that deals with chaotic markets and survival strategies.

Dr. Samli has worked with hundreds of small- and medium-sized businesses as a consultant, over a 40-year period. Dr. Samli has given many seminars before hundreds of business managers in Turkey, Australia, Norway, New Zealand, and other parts of the world.

Dr. Samli has had more than 20,000 students from all over the world. Many of them are professors, successful businessmen, and statesmen. He reviews dissertations as an outside international expert.